DEATH CAME CALLING
BUT I WASN T HOME

DEATH CAME CALLING BUT I WASN'T HOME

Floyd Schneider

Keybobby
Books

Spokane, WA 99223

Published by Keybobby Books, a division of Tradewinds West, LLC
Spokane, WA 99223.
www.floydschneider.com

Library of Congress Cataloging-in-Publication Data

Schneider, Floyd E.
   Death Came Calling, But I Wasn't Home / Floyd E Schneider —
First edition.
        pages.cm
   ISBN 978-1-64633-201-4 (paperback)
Vietnam War, 1961-1975 -- Personal narratives, American
DS557.S36453 2019

First Edition 2019

Cover designed by Ira-Rebeca from rebecacovers.

Printing in the United States of America 2019

Disclaimer

I have changed some of the names of people in this book because I was not able to find them to ask for their approval of to include them in this book. I have attempted to recall as accurately as possible the people, events and things I have described in this book.

DEDICATION

First, to Christine, who has encouraged me all along to make this book better and better by editing, editing, editing. I know that she found it difficult to help me, since she was nervous about causing conflict between us, if I chose to reject her opinion at times. Although she refrained from saying everything she wanted to say, she never gave up gently pushing me to edit more. She is the best wife and editor God could have ever given me.

Second, to Kay Tronsen for her endless editing and her constant tears every time she finished reading the book.

Third, Wayne, for making my time in the Army and in Vietnam better than it would have been, had he not been there.

Fourth, to my children, grandchildren, inlaws, and all the students who have tolerated my stories about my time in Vietnam. I'm certain that I have related some events to them that did not make it into this book due to a failing memory.

Contents

PREFACE

I'm writing this book for my two sons, two daughters-in-law, and eight grandchildren. They already know a lot about my combat experience, but now they can quote me. Over time I've forgotten lots of events and details. I've tried to be as accurate as my failing memory will allow. I've changed most of the names of my fellow soldiers in combat, since I have not been able to contact them about the accuracy of my memory.

I was almost seven years into my journey with Jesus when I went to Vietnam. I disobeyed regularly, but somehow managed to keep from damaging myself permanently. I believe that He chose to protect me from myself. Yes, He protected this disobedient follower from the evil and suffering from others, but I was, and am, my own worst enemy.

The big question others have asked me, about myself and about themselves: Why did some die and others live? Why did I not die? After a firefight, soldiers asked themselves that question, and then died in the next firefight. Why?

I've answered that question for myself. Hope you can find the answer soon.

1. MAY, 1966: FREEDOM REMOVED

Few people choose how they die. When soldiers go to war, they plan on returning home, whether they volunteered or were drafted. Over fifty thousand men did not return home alive from the Vietnam war.

The government sent every eligible male a number, and when the wheels of bureaucracy called up your number, you gleefully showed up at your appointed Induction Center of your military branch. Governments authorize a draft when more men are needed for a war than want to join the military. The United States has drafted men into the military for seven wars: the American Revolution, the American Civil War, World War I, World War II, the Cold War, the Korean War and the Vietnam War. The draft ceased in 1973, but a "Selective Service System" still exists as a contingency plan if the overall security of America is threatened.

The Vietnam War required a lot of soldiers. Apart from making the military your life career or joining the CIA, the Army offered us two options for fighting the war against Communism. We consented (as opposed to escaping to Canada) to be drafted for two years of active duty, followed by four years of active reserve (digging foxholes one weekend a month for four years), or we enlisted as an RA, Regular Army, for three years active service and three years of inactive reserve (no obligations to attend any monthly drills).

I enlisted.

How did that happen?

Toward the very end of my last semester in high school I spoke with my high school principal about college. He told me that I wasn't serious enough about college. He said I would probably flunk out of college at this point in my life. I asked for an alternative. He felt the military was a good option for me. I don't think he even thought about the war in Vietnam at that point.

I went to a Navy recruiter and asked if I could drive submarines. Does one "drive" submarines? He said no, because I wore glasses. I asked an Air Force recruiter if I could fly fighter jets, and he said no, because I wore glasses. I asked an Army recruiter if I could jump out of airplanes, even though I wore glasses, and he said, "Sign here!"

On graduation evening, everyone dressed up and took their dates out for the big party after graduation. Mark, one of my close friends, and I had decided to join the Army together, and we double-dated as well. We took our dates to the dance, and as the dancing wound down, everyone descended on all the local attractions in St. Francis, Kansas. All the business owners in town generously opened their stores and shops for the graduating seniors from Thursday evening until 6 a.m. Friday morning. And everything was free. Bowling, ice cream shop, movie theatre. We had the run of the town. We lost count of the number of times that we drove up and down main street until we delivered our dates home at 6 a.m. It was the only all-night date I had ever been on, but I didn't even get a free goodbye kiss.

On Monday morning, Mark and I were on a bus to Ft. Bliss, Texas. High school was over! Freedom! I was a moron. Basic Training. May, June, and July. In the desert. I'm really intelligent sometimes. This wasn't one of those times.

We arrived and discovered immediately that the drill sergeant's main function focused on eliminating any and all independent thinking.

"You will do exactly as you are told! You will obey every order immediately and exactly as it is given!"

The platoon sergeant impressed upon his ignorant charges the privilege of being a squad leader. He chose his minions based on their personal initiative, which contradicted the drill sergeant's speech about independent thinking.

I don't know what I did wrong, but after the first week, my platoon sergeant gave me the privilege of being a squad leader. Actually, he gave me more opportunities for more people to cause me more problems.

During the second or third week, they told us that we had an hour to prepare for an inspection in the barracks. Beds made perfectly, no wrinkles, clothes lined up, everything super clean and neat. Weapons cleaned without a speck of anything on them. One guy in my squad forgot to put the cleaning rod through the barrel of his weapon one last time. The sergeant found one small spot on the inside of the barrel. My entire squad got the weekend off, but as the squad leader who was responsible for his squad, I ended up in the kitchen on kitchen duty (KP). I wasn't upset. I was relieved that my punishment hadn't been worse, although I'm not sure what that would have looked like.

I arrived in the kitchen at 6 a.m. The head cook put me on pots and pans. A few minutes later a recruit from Puerto Rico joined me. His English was first-grade level. I have no idea how he got in the Army, but we laughed and bonded over our language ineptness. I wished that I hadn't needed to cheat on the final exam of my high school Spanish class.

Basic Training taught me how to defend myself, one-on-one. I didn't seek out any bullies, but I felt more confident. I had learned to avoid starting something that I couldn't finish. My dad had taught me that if someone wanted to hurt me, and if I couldn't get away, then the rules went out the window. He gave me permission to do anything to win as quickly as possible. Plan ahead if possible but end it quickly and get away. Don't hang around and gloat. Arrogance was stupid. Just leave. Life was too short to spend fighting unnecessarily.

At 71, I wonder why some things stick in my memory. One man in our unit was mentally challenged. He was the sweetest person ever. He so wanted to make it through Basic Training, but the government should have been charged with criminal activity for allowing him to enlist. Our drill sergeant was a drill sergeant. He never, never smiled. He yelled a lot. The Army probably gave him his job because of his vocal cords.

One morning, as we all lined up for inspection, that nice

young man came out of the barracks with two left boots on. The drill sergeant stepped up to his face and ordered him to go back into the barracks and come down with different boots on. He returned to the barracks. A few minutes later, he came down with two right boots on. It was the only time that we saw the sergeant almost lose it. A minuscule smile crept onto his lips and betrayed his incredible self-control. I think he gently sent the young man to the captain. I don't remember seeing him again. They probably sent him home. I'm sure that he was devastated, but it's a lie to believe that a person can be anything they want to be. I wanted to drive submarines.

Some parts of basic training wiped out some of the guys. The sergeants treated those more harshly who did poorly. I managed to stay invisible. I passed everything, although never excelled at much, except on the gunnery range. I almost felt at home.

Safeway gave me my first rifle. When I was ten, Safeway Gold Bond Stamps rewarded customers with a catalog full of practical things, like kitchen items, garden supplies and guns. It was my dad's turn to exchange the stamps for whatever he wanted. When I saw the new catalog, I couldn't believe my eyes. We had just filled out the six books of stamps, and what I wanted cost six books exactly. I begged dad to let me use those stamps next. I even promised to be a good boy and to skip my next turn. I showed him what I wanted in the catalog. He smiled and nodded approval. Mom saw what I wanted and frowned.

We all three went down to Safeway and I turned in the six books of stamps. The manager asked me what I wanted. I pointed to the item in the catalog. He smiled, took the stamps and the catalog and disappeared into the back of the store. When he returned, I could hardly control myself.

He placed in my hands a Remington, single-action, single-shot, bolt action .22 rifle that fired long-rifle bullets. Dad beamed. Mom frowned. Dad handed me a box of .22 long-rifle bullets and told me to never use short rounds, or it would jam, and that I could go out into one of the fields outside of town to practice. I could shoot cans and rocks and anything but people or domestic animals. Mom frowned some more.

Dad told her, "He has to start sometime."

"He's only ten," she replied.

"You're from Texas and you're worried about your ten-year-old son using a small .22?"

She worried. Mom loved me.

I brought a rabbit home for supper. The only reason I hit him was because he had to have been 200 years old and couldn't move very fast. He was so tough that Mom couldn't tenderize him enough to make a meal out of him. She was a great cook, but that rabbit was beyond her skill.

I even earned my Boy Scout merit badge for marksmanship with that rifle. I wore glasses, but the sights were dead on. Once dad taught me how to squeeze the trigger instead of jerking it. I hit my target more often and used less ammo. We weren't rich. Ammo was expensive.

Dad and I cycled through a number of other rifles, but all were .22s. The nicest one was a Remington Model 12 pump-action. It held seven rounds in the magazine tube that slid back with the pump whenever you wanted to load another round into the chamber. It fired shorts, longs, and long-rifle rounds.

We tried a semi-automatic once. You didn't need to manually load another round in the chamber; you just had to pull the trigger. I had developed the very bad habit of pulling the trigger again after firing my own .22. I did that with the automatic and put a round just about a foot over my dad's head. He sold the automatic the next day. I stopped the habit immediately.

I never warmed up to handguns until I entered the Army. The training we received with the Springfield .45 was just short of pathetic, but that couldn't be helped. It takes a lot of practice to hit something with a handgun. Jerking the trigger, instead of squeezing it, will pull the muzzle a millimeter to the right, and you'll miss the burglar six feet away and kill your neighbor across the street. You have a better chance of defending yourself by throwing the .45 at your attacker.

The first time I stepped onto the rifle range in Basic Training, I felt in control. I immediately realized that an M16 worked the same way that any of the .22 caliber rifles worked that I had used growing up. Same procedure. Take a breath and hold it. Squeeze the trigger, don't pull it. I just had to practice doing it faster. I got almost perfect scores with the M60, the M14 and the M16.

Firing a perfect score garnered my E-7 sergeant high prestige with his superiors. I was elated when my E-5 scornfully told me that I looked too much like a runt to be carrying the M60, no matter how high my target scores. "What good's a perfect score if you can't carry the damn thing!"

Perfection was mandatory on the grenade range. Although our unit never experienced such an incident, the drill sergeants told us about "mistakes" (fill in descriptive cuss words here) that recruits had made during grenade practice. The sergeant would stand on the edge of the grenade pit while the recruit threw the grenade down range.

When the soldiers were placed in the grenade pit for learning how to throw a grenade, they were told to hold the grenade in their throwing hand, pull the pin with their other hand, and throw the grenade as far out of the hole as they could with their throwing hand. One soldier thought that he was supposed to drop the pin first, before throwing the grenade. He climbed down into the pit, and the sergeant handed him the grenade. The recruit was told to do it. He put the grenade in his right hand, pulled the pin with his left hand, dropped the grenade in the pit and threw the pin down range. While screaming, "Grenade!", the sergeant reached down into the pit, grabbed the recruit by his shirt and yanked him out of the pit and fell on him. The grenade made the pit a bit deeper. That recruit was recycled through another grenade practice lesson.

I did not experience any bliss during Basic Training at Ft.

Bliss, Texas, in May, June and July. I should've waited until fall. The forced march through the desert, toward the end of that eight weeks, raised the experience of pain to its highest level so far. Before beginning the march, we shouldered our equipment and weapons and stood around a lot. The heat from the sand burned through my boots. I couldn't stand still for more than a few seconds. Once the march started, single file, I remember repeating over and over to myself, "Just take the next step. Just take the next step." We passed a couple of guys who had fallen out from heat exhaustion. I kept hoping that the guy in front of me didn't fall out, because I wasn't sure if I was supposed to stop and help him or end up on KP duty for being accused of helping him to keep from having to finish the march. Slowly, my numbed mind lost track of anybody else. I might have slept while walking. Then I felt a difference in my boots. The soft sand had changed to hard ground. Pavement. I had made it. Those who fell out got KP during the weekend. I doubt anyone complained after that march.

We made it through that training thinking that we had survived something horrendous. The torments of Basic Training would turn out to be insignificant compared to combat. I'm not sure even seasoned veterans can prepare newcomers for reality. A new recruit might have to live through a firefight before he realizes what he has to do to stay alive. One never knows how one will respond when the bullets start flying.

Graduation, a parade, the American Flag, lots of salutes and speeches, honors for achievements that were meant to inspire a soldier to work harder on his next assignment, stripes to signify advancement in rank to Private First Class (one upside down gold "V" on each sleeve). Then everyone lined up to get their orders. A few had to go through parts of Basic Training again. They stayed at Ft. Bliss. Most were sent to the training they had signed up for. I was being sent to Ft. Ord, California, for AIT, Advanced Infantry Training. I had signed up to jump out of planes. Basic Training just informed you that you were in the Army. The real training hadn't started yet.

The Army gave me a two-week vacation. My stepdad, Bill, and Mom had moved to Colorado while I was at Boot Camp. I took the bus to Longmont to be with Mom. I had not been very nice to her during my senior year. She had done everything for me, but I hadn't seen it yet. I was still being a brat. A jerk. I should have apologized to her, but I hadn't realized how much I had hurt her, nor how much she had worried that I might have stopped loving her. It still hurts to think about that time. We got along fine, but I just wish I had been mature enough to not have put her through that needless suffering.

Advanced Infantry Training
Ft. Ord, CA

I arrived at Ft. Ord, California, in early August. The weather was deceptive. It lulled me into believing that combat would be like training. Ft. Ord was the jewel of the US Army. Sand dunes and forests along the coast of Monterey Bay. From the desert of west Texas in July to the blue water of the Pacific in August was like moving from hell to heaven. At the height of Fort Ord's activity, some 50,000 troops passed through that base on their way to the Vietnam and Korean Wars.

I ended up being a squad leader again. I'm not sure how that happened. I really didn't want the job. I was fine taking orders. I hadn't run into any incompetent sergeants or officers yet.

The captain called in all the squad leaders from each platoon to give us a speech about leadership. He had each one of us introduce ourselves. After my short introduction, his eyes opened wide as he leaned back in his chair and mumbled, "Whoo. You just got out of high school?" It wasn't a question.

I nodded.

All the other squad leaders had had some college before joining or getting drafted. I got lucky. After that meeting, our platoon sergeant lined us up outside beside an unfinished trench and asked how many had some college education. A few raised their hands. The sergeant pointed down toward some shovels in trench. "You guys can use your college education to teach us how to dig trenches." I'm not sure if the sergeant had even graduated from high school.

One guy in my squad wanted my position as squad leader. He wouldn't follow any of my orders. I wanted to give him my position, but the platoon sergeant said no. When the sergeant spoke to him about his attitude, that young soldier mouthed off to the sergeant. That soldier spent more time shoveling dirt in the trenches than all the college-educated guys combined. Then he did hundreds of push-ups.

On one combat exercise, I was ordered to take my squad straight through a tree-lined open area to search for the enemy. Right out in the open. Dumb. No one told us that the tree line defined the perimeter of the exercise area. I sent half my squad along the tree line, telling them to avoid the open area as much as possible, and I took the other half with me through that tree line. There was nobody on the other side of the tree line. We moved away from the tree line and crouched our way around some dunes.

When we stuck our heads up over the sand dunes and looked back, we discovered that we had outflanked the enemy. With the proper hand signals, we hunched down behind the dunes, loaded the blank rounds into our M16, and then I ordered my men to charge the enemy killing everyone in sight.

It wasn't my fault. I thought they were the enemy. The enemy was still waiting in the trees for half of my squad, who were not walking out in the open, but were sneaking along the tree line. They never connected with each other. With a burst of five M16s firing on fully automatic, my half of the squad had theoretically obliterated a handful of unaware officers who were standing at a distance with their backs to us overseeing the exercise. I think they peed their pants.

The sergeant demanded to know why I had not proceeded as directed. I don't remember my exact words, but he only grunted when I explained how stupid it was to search for the enemy by staying out in the open. I think they were testing us to see how we would react if we were ambushed. They didn't react well.

I excelled in small arms, again. My platoon sergeant, as usual, got lots of credit for my achievements. I was put in charge of a squad with one M60 machine gun attached to it. Toward the end of that eight weeks, I was asked if I wanted to attend OCS, Officer Candidate School. I said yes, and I was put on a waiting list. They took men first who did not wear glasses. I waited eight weeks for my orders, which never came. Now that I think about it, if I hadn't gotten bored and impatient, I probably could have stayed at Ft. Ord until my enlistment ran out.

I had almost nothing to do, but I enjoyed that eight weeks. I bought a 1952 Chevy, so I wasn't stuck with public transportation. I had taken SCUBA lessons in Denver when I was in high school. I hooked up with a SCUBA diving club comprised of an ex-policeman, a couple of hippies, an attorney, among others, all of whom were far more experienced in diving than I was. One weekend, we drove to Carmel Beach and dove right off the beach.

I remember being in about twenty feet of water, looking down and seeing a huge monster fish, five feet long, just off the beach. I watched it move and settle a few feet away. My eyes were glued to that thing. Then, all of a sudden, it moved again, back to its original position. I was hoping that it wouldn't look up, see me, and decide to choose me for lunch. My shiver rippled through the water.

Then it moved a third time, back to the same spot it had just come from. It took me a few seconds to register that it was just a large five-foot rock, and that I was moving. The emotionless tide had tricked me. I didn't tell any of the club members. They weren't really polite people.

Another time, we dove south of Carmel Beach, but we

had to swim around a huge patch of seaweed before descending to the bottom at seventy feet. We had an odd number of divers that day, so a couple more experienced divers added me as a third partner. I hadn't told them that I needed extra time to clear my ears around ten feet before descending further, and when they looked back and saw me hesitate, they assumed I was afraid, and motioned for me to stay on the top until they returned. They didn't want to be left behind by the other guys. No hard feelings. I didn't want to spoil their dive by being a novice.

I made it back around the seaweed patch, and as I reached the beach, I saw the entire group surface where I had come from. One diver was holding an extra tank, and two others were keeping a fourth diver afloat on his back. Something had gone wrong with his heart just as they reached the bottom, but another diver noticed it, and the team saved his life. I then recalled diving alone just off the beach a couple weeks before. At night. I wasn't very bright at nineteen. I didn't brag about that dive, and I never dove alone again.

My car broke down at one point, and I had to walk back to the base. I was in uniform, and I entered an area of large green lawns. I had no idea where I was. I remember someone yelling, "Fore!", but I was still clueless. I'm not sure when I realized that I had walked all the way across Pebble Beach Golf Course.

I spent time in the base library. As I perused titles on the shelves, my eyes were jarred by the title of one book, *God is Dead*. I pulled the book off the shelf and read the first chapter. Paul Tillich wrote about God as the Ground of Being. I had no idea who Tillich was, but I felt sorry for him. I assumed that he was a highly educated professor (who else would write such books), but he clearly had no personal relationship with his creator, who wanted a very personal relationship with him. I checked out a spy novel. It probably had more truth in it than Tillich's book.

When I said that I had almost nothing to do, I still got posted on guard duty. My name surfaced on the roster for the guard tower at the local Army prison. I spent eight hours watching inmates come outside the kitchen area during their breaks and smoke. Some rolled banana peels into the cigarette wrappers and smoked more than just tobacco. I waved at most of them. I could see their smiles, and we made signs with each other about exchanging cigarettes or drinking a beer.

Then the bottom fell out.

Bill, my stepdad, called. Mom was in the hospital. The doctor wasn't saying that things would be all right. Without stating it directly, he had made it clear that she was going to die.

When my Mom was nine years old, she fell ill to rheumatic fever which weakened her heart. The doctor told her that she would die if she ever gave birth to a child. At eighteen, she eloped. Not really intelligent, but my existence is founded on her rebellion. She only had one child: me.

Sometimes we lived below the poverty line, and sometimes above it, and Mom had to work as a waitress all the time. However, she never made me feel like we were poor. I seldom saw her frown, and the truckers loved her humor. They would drive fifty miles out of the way in the middle of their night runs just to have her serve them coffee.

It wasn't always pleasant for her, and she had to keep her guard up. One time a trucker tried to grab her, but he made the mistake of doing so while he was still sitting in the booth. He had grabbed her waist with his right hand and had placed his left hand on the table in order to push himself up. Mom rammed a fork into his left hand and the fork pinned his hand to the table. The other truckers cheered for her. Another time two burly truckers hauled an unruly trucker out back behind the restaurant and beat him up for groping Mom. They let everyone know that Mom was the only bright spot on their late-night runs.

When I was in the ninth grade, Dad had gotten fired again, which usually happened every six months. I had just begun to make friends, as a teenager, and the prospect of moving again devastated me. I had been getting straight A's, getting beat up on the football field, but not by bullies in the back alleys. Life was great. Dad got fired. I quit.

The math teacher, our freshman football coach, called Mom into his office. He told her that he had never seen a kid go from straight A's to straight D's overnight. Then he added that something was wrong at that kid's home, and that if that kid's parents didn't get their act together, they were going to destroy that kid.

I couldn't have understood at the time, but that conversation had devastated Mom. We moved, and I entered the middle of my freshman year in St. Francis, Kansas.

The summer of 1962 changed all of our lives. It began as a heavenly summer. I was washing dishes in three restaurants for my own pocket change when Mom's boss asked if I wanted to work with her during the night shift. It paid a lot more than those three part-time day-jobs. The cook took me under her wing and taught me how to cook everything on the menu. She was really sweet. After the first week, she left and never came back. I spent the summer cooking and washing dishes, and Mom brought in the tips. The truckers kept telling me how fortunate I was to have such a Mom.

Children go through hell when their parents get divorced. Dad held that job barely six months, and then demanded that we all leave and move to his new job in Wyoming. Mom had had enough. She informed him that she and I were staying in St. Francis until I graduated from high school. Dad issued his usual order to obey his command. He left town, expecting us to follow within the week. After eighteen years of a rocky marriage, Mom filed for divorce. It was messy. Before the summer was over, dad was sending letters blaming everybody else for the divorce, including me. Mom tried to protect me from his attacks, but I had to grow up someday. I cried some, but only Jesus kept me from retaliating against his accusations toward me and Mom.

Once the word got out that Mom was getting divorced,

the offers of marriage poured in. This thirty-three year-old gorgeous red-headed Irish-Texas woman had captured the hearts of everybody in town and on the road. She told me later that she knew she couldn't support both of us on waitress pay, so she prayed to Jesus that He would give her a husband who was a follower of Jesus and who was kind. God honored her prayer, and I benefited from it by getting one of the best stepdads in the world: Bill Reynolds. Bill was well accepted in the community, and high school, in that small town, became tolerable. Hell faded as I entered a heavenly period of limited acceptance by the semi-marginalized fringe in town.

I regret the spring semester of my senior year, 1966. Mom and I fought. I was trying to grow up and be an adult. I was driving with her in the car one day, and I started arguing with her about something. I could see that she was fighting tears, but I didn't understand why.

Then she mumbled to herself, "I thought I was doing the best for you by keeping you in one place for high school." I wish I had understood what was going on in her mind then. At eighteen, I arrogantly assumed a lot of wrong stuff, and I hurt her deeply.

And now she was dying, and my meanness to her had come full circle. I hadn't apologized to her. I wanted to die. I cried and prayed during my entire shift of eight hours in the guard tower. When the next soldier came to relieve me, I told him to take a break and that I would stand guard for him. He saw the tears and quietly left. I cried and prayed for another eight hours.

Mom couldn't die. Not yet. I owed her an apology. I did love her. I needed to tell her that. She was the only person in the world I was consciously willing to die for. How could I have been so selfish and so cruel? I was her only son, her only child. I wasn't a bad person. How could I have treated her like that? How could I have ever let her believe that I would desert her? After all she had done for me?

I was bone tired when I came out of the guard tower. My sergeant met me at the gate. He pulled me aside and handed me a paper. I read it. It was leave papers to go home. The return date was left blank. I was still fighting the emotions of Mom's possible death, so I wasn't sure how to respond. The Army doesn't normally treat soldiers with that much grace. All I remember the sergeant saying was, "Don't forget to come back when this is over." I was so consumed with my own misery, that I still don't remember his name.

I arrived in Denver the next day wearing civilian clothes. When I called Bill, he wasn't answering the telephone, so I went straight to the hospital. Bill wasn't there either. I asked someone about Mom. They told me her room number, but that she was unconscious and that I couldn't see her until I had spoken with the doctor.

But what if she died before . . .?

Bill and I finally connected and drove home. I don't think he had eaten or slept in three days. Neither of us talked about it. He was the best stepdad I could have ever had. Not because of how he treated me, which was good, but because of how he treated my one and only Mom.

The next day we arrived together. We spoke with the doctor. Mom was awake, and although we could speak with her, she wasn't able to talk yet. Bill and I saw her together, then Bill allowed me to speak with her alone. I said everything I wanted to say, and more. I cried. I squeezed her hand the entire time. I begged her to not die. Mom never said a word, but she smiled. Finally, a nurse nudged me out. Bill and I went home, still not talking about it.

The next morning the doctor met us at the nurses' station. Bill and I both hoped for the best, but we had expected the worst. The doctor wasn't smiling, but then he wasn't frowning like someone who was about to deliver some devastating news. He just looked perplexed.

He shook his head. "I have no idea what's going on. Some things just can't be explained by medicine. I saw your Willene two days ago, just before she slipped into what we thought was a coma. It was as if she didn't want to live. Everything wrong with her should come from having a weak heart . . .."

I nodded. He looked at me with a question mark on his face. I said, "Mom had rheumatic fever when she was nine years old, and it weakened her heart."

He knew that from her record. He nodded, and said, "But her heart isn't that bad yet. She shouldn't be anywhere near dying."

Bill spoke, "So what are you saying?"

The doctor, still looking perplexed, said, "It seems that two days ago she wanted to die. This morning she is wide awake and wants to go home. I still want to run couple of tests on her, but it looks like you can take her home tomorrow."

Self-control keeps a person from making a complete fool of oneself. I did not cry or scream for joy at that point. After she arrived home, and got her voice back, I got my chance to re-apologize to Mom and assure her of my love. She hugged me for so long. Maybe I'm being too sentimental, but I don't believe any mom and son could have been more bonded than we were. From that point on, I would have done anything for her.

Much later I asked Mom about my talk with her in the room alone. She said she didn't remember it. She really loved Bill, and he deserved her. Although one time I accused her of loving me more than Bill, but she just smiled and put her finger to her lips.

I returned to Ft. Ord and thanked the sergeant for his favor, but I still don't remember his name.

~~~~

The war was raging in Vietnam, and I was still waiting for my orders for OCS. After two months of being a tourist in Monterey and Carmel, I got seriously bored. After the near-death drowning, the SCUBA guys met too erratically, and the small library ran out of interesting books for someone who had been trained for combat.

I inquired about joining the Green Beret, just to get some orders sooner than later. They gave me a couple of tests and told me that I could shift from OCS to their training school. That day I inquired again about my OCS orders, and the sergeant mentioned that once I was accepted in OCS and started that training, I would have to spend a minimum time (two years, three years?) in the Army after graduation. That minimum time could possibly take me beyond my three-year enlistment. And the sergeant told me that I might be on the waiting list for months before my orders came through. Apparently, we weren't losing enough second lieutenants in Vietnam yet. It never occurred to me that I might be able to miss out on Vietnam entirely by waiting months to get my orders for OCS, change my mind and turn them down, and go back to waiting for orders to Vietnam. They didn't send you to Nam if you had less than twelve months enlistment left.

That day I did some serious thinking. OCS or the Green Beret, after waiting an indefinite time at Ft. Ord, would probably mean longer than three years in the Army. Was that what I really wanted to do with my life? I went back to the original plan. The sergeant cancelled my requests for OCS and Green Beret training, and I shipped out the next day for Ft. Benning, GA, Jump School.

When I arrived at Benning, I noticed a lot of pretty, and young ladies outside the gate, all talking and chatting and waiting for something. I got off the bus last, and the bus driver saw me looking at the ladies. I was a bit taken aback by his disgust as he snorted. He asked me if I was going into the airborne or OCS? I hadn't realized that both training schools were held at Ft. Benning. I said Jump School.

He replied, "That's good. You won't be accosted by those gold diggers."

I had no idea what a gold digger was. I asked.

"Those young ladies are trying to find themselves a new second lieutenant to marry, in hopes that he will get killed in Vietnam so they can collect the $10,000 life insurance policy for the widow." I chose not to believe him. I chose to believe that bitterness had consumed him because of some previous bad experience.

I had arrived one week early. The sergeant in charge asked me to lay low and stay out of trouble. I didn't see him for the rest of the week.

During Airborne training, we ran. And ran. And ran. I loved running. The platoon sergeant woke us up very early every morning. Those who attempted to sleep later than allowed ran more, did more push-ups and cleaned toilets with no breaks. Few guys chose to sleep late.

I still love to run. At 71, I have acquired two titanium replacement knees which force me to walk instead. I miss running, but at least I'm not crawling.

Just before our last week of training, we all had to jump off the 250-foot tower. I climbed the stairs, strapped on the harness, adjusted it so it wouldn't castrate me when the chute opened, hooked onto the static line, and jumped off the platform. Some guys threw up. None of the sergeants stood directly under the tower. Some guys sniffled tears. Most of us wanted to do it again. Our training time didn't allow more than one jump per person.

The third week we jumped from planes once a day for five days. We got up early (as usual), ate breakfast (always good food), got suited up with everything we needed to jump, then stood out on the airport tarmac for two to four hours, usually running in place or doing push-ups, and always checking and re-checking our gear. The drill sergeants continually painted detailed pictures of what would happen to us if we made the slightest mistake. Broken skulls, an invalid for life, not able to satisfy our wives in bed. An endless list of tragic endings. Then they asked if anyone wanted to step to the side and be re-assigned to a less dangerous unit. Some always did.

We climbed into the C-130 turboprops, sat down facing each other across the aisle and waited until the green light went on. The jumpmaster gave the order to stand up and hook up. We grabbed our static lines that automatically pulled our chutes open when we jumped, and clipped them onto the steel cable that ran from the front to the back of the plane just above our heads.

We jumped out of the side doors and right into the prop blast, which slammed into me and hurled me away from the plane and from the next guy jumping out. I could see the sky, the ground, and guy in front of me as his chute opened up, and I felt like I was part of something important. Then reality returned when my chute popped open and the straps slammed my nuts into my rib cage, even if I had set the harness properly. After the first jump, I realized that the pain of the chute opening was preferable to the chute not opening. That chute kept me alive.

Once the pain had subsided, I began to notice how many white balloons were floating toward the earth, each carrying enough firepower to overcome anything on the ground. Most of the men were quiet, some were yelling in exhilaration, some were pulling on their risers just for the fun of it. As I twirled around, the checkered countryside, waterways, and tiny little indistinguishable buildings spread out beneath me from horizon to horizon. I belonged up there floating in the air. Then I realized that I wasn't floating; I was falling. The serenity of the abstract became the realism of the hard ground as it charged toward my very small frame.

I would either land in the DZ (drop zone) or I wouldn't. I either would make a good roll when I hit the ground or I wouldn't, which usually jarred every bone in my body. More pain. I would either quickly release my parachute or I wouldn't, which could drag me a few feet before depositing me in a heap or dropping me into a ditch, which could break my neck.

Then I looked up. The next wave of billowing mushrooms opened and descended toward the earth. How could I not love this life?

The first time I jumped was automatic. Exhilarating. The second time, for some reason, I hesitated for a split second and a sergeant's heavy boot kicked me out the door.

One thousand feet up. Not much time for mistakes. If my parachute didn't open, I used my reserve chute. It fit snuggly on my stomach. If my main chute didn't open up, or if it did open, but it turned itself into a cigarette roll instead of a white billowing cloud above my head, I was supposed to place my left hand on the reserve chute, press the chute hard against my stomach, pull the reserve's rip cord with my right hand, and then slam my right fist back into the right side of the reserve chute to make sure that it opened up in front of me and didn't slither up and wrap around my cigarette-rolled main chute.

It was never foolproof. When one of the trainers jumped out, his main chute slithered out and snaked its way past his head into a cigarette roll. When he pulled the rip cord on his reserve, he forgot to slam his fist into the reserve, and it just kind of fell out forward, and then the air current threw it straight up past his face, and it wrapped itself around his main chute. He grabbed the lines of the main chute and spent those few seconds violently shaking them and cussing at them. He hit the ground, hard. He didn't die. Just broke his leg. The next day his story got around to everyone. When he asked the doctor why he had not died, the doctor told him that cussing out his chute had kept his mind off the ground, and, therefore, his body was relaxed, not rigid, when it hit the ground. The doctor said that if he had been thinking about hitting the ground, he would have shattered every bone in his body. The moral of the story was to always be ready to cuss out your chute if it didn't open properly.

Christmas: I received some Christmas cards and a box of candy from Mom. We talked lots on the phone. I didn't tell her about the trainer's chute not opening. I graduated and received orders for the 101st Airborne Division, Ft. Campbell, KY. No leave granted. I arrived at Ft. Campbell the next week. I never expected that my first combat experience might occur in the Middle East or in Detroit, Michigan.

2. JANUARY, 1967: ALMOST FIRST COMBAT

I arrived in January, 1967, at Ft. Campbell, Kentucky (not Tennessee). Though ninety percent of the base was located in Tennessee, the government had placed the Post Office just north of the Kentucky state line, so despite actually being in Tennessee, I was in Kentucky, according to the government. Fun times.

I was posted to Company A of the 502nd Infantry Regiment of the First Battalion of the First Brigade of the Screaming Eagles, the 101st Airborne Division. I had no idea what life was supposed to be like once a soldier had finished with all of his initial training.

Well, more training, of course!

I met Wayne. It was really uncanny. We clicked immediately. We could almost read each others' thoughts. Someone would say something across the room, and we would both start laughing. We were in the same platoon. We spent all our free time together, except when Wayne went home to spend a weekend with his girlfriend, Diane. She was a beautiful Southern Bell. Elegant, graceful, funny. I wasn't interested in marriage yet, but if she had dumped Wayne and asked me to marry her, I probably would have said yes.

There were very few true followers of Jesus in our unit. Diane was a follower of Jesus, but Wayne had not moved in that direction yet. I hounded him with stories about Jesus. I look back and realize that I should apologize for my abrupt approach, but we had become such good friends so quickly, that neither of us minded the challenge. I think I even told Diane that she shouldn't marry him because he had not given his life to Jesus yet, and that although there was no romantic love between us, she had a better chance of a good marriage if she married me. She told me that she was counting on me to influence Wayne in the right direction. I wasn't going to let her off by placing that burden on me, so I verbally rejected her request to influence Wayne, but I never gave up trying anyway.

I was awarded E-4 while at Ft. Campbell, and a sergeant talked me out of taking a three-day flame-thrower course. Sometimes I listened to the advice of others.

In May and June, 1967, the Middle East exploded. Our platoon sergeants intensified the drills, and something had changed. During our first A-drill, the sergeant ordered us to pack our personal belongings in one bag and stuff it in our lockers until the drill was over. We then took our equipment outside and marched around a lot. Then the B-drills began. The sergeant told us to put our home addresses on our bags that contained our personal belongings. Then each squad and platoon jettisoned any unnecessary equipment, taking just the combat gear needed to engage in direct combat. Trucks drove to the woods, and we practiced coordinated attacks against an invisible enemy and marched around a lot. That non-existent enemy kept us busy from early morning until late in the evening.

Then, one morning, the sergeant announced a C-drill. He told us to pack our personal bags with our home addresses and write a goodbye letter to whomever was going to receive the bags. We had never heard of C-drills.

We packed our bags, wrote those letters, sealed them, and put them in our bags. The supply sergeant handed each of us live ammunition with our weapons. As we left the building, we were handed parachutes and told to put them on. Normally, we drove to the hanger to pick up our chutes for our regular practice jumps. This wasn't a regular practice jump. They put us in trucks—no marching—and drove us to the airport. Completely outfitted for a combat jump, we climbed aboard some C-141 aircrafts for a flight to somewhere. One didn't fly just across the state line in a C-141. We were obviously heading overseas. And we were combat troops. This is what we had been trained for.

I was too young and inexperienced to be afraid of what

was coming. I hadn't seen the death of friends yet. I hadn't felt the bullets whiz inches past my head or watched mortar rounds spread body parts all over the trees. We sat shoulder to shoulder crammed into our seats, our chutes forcing us to sit leaning forward, holding onto nothing with our left hands and clenching our static lines in our right hands. When the order came, we would stand up, turn ninety degrees toward the door, reach up and hook up our static line to the long cable attached to the inside of the plane. When the green light blinked, each man would jump out the door with no hesitation so the next guy in line didn't jump into the parachute in front of him.

After sitting scrunched together like a package of hotdogs, the engines started up. The propellers were deafening. We waited for the jerk of the first forward movement. Over the rumble and din, the officer inside the aircraft yelled to tell us to "lock and load" our weapons, put them on safety and wait for instructions to hook up our static line.

Everybody fed a clip of M16 ammunition into the magazine chamber, loaded a round into the chamber, clicked on the safety button. This was no drill. This was live. If we flew somewhere and jumped out, the officer would tell us who to shoot on the way down, assuming we made it to the ground. Probably anybody that didn't have a 101st Screaming Eagle white patch on their shoulder.

(I often wondered about the visibility of that very white patch to the enemy. An officer in Vietnam once ordered us to stop smearing mud on the patch for less visibility. He said that we needed to show pride in our unit by displaying the patch. We wanted to ask him to lead the way with his white patch screaming, "Here I am! Shoot me!" We kept it clean on the base, and smeared mud on it in the field.)

We didn't lift off immediately. All of the "hurry up and wait" gave us time to think about what might be going on. The logic was obvious. This wasn't a training exercise. If they were sending us to set up some kind of base camp, we wouldn't need our parachutes. We were going to jump in "hot," directly into a war zone. The engine noise hindered us from discussing our assumptions, but our speculations ran wild. Would we receive fire from the ground before we even exited the plane? Were we being dropped right into the middle of a firefight? Who were we supposed to shoot? Would we have the time to form our squads into our elite fighting units, or was it every man for himself until somebody won the battle? What kind of communications would we have once we left the plane? We would resort to the original orders: jump out and shoot anybody that didn't have our white patch on their sleeve.

The green light never went on. The officer yelled, "We're standing down!" He ordered us to stand up and file out of the plane. The engines and propellers wound down. Trucks took us back to the barracks. We turned in our gear, unpacked our bags, overjoyed that no one had sent off our love letters.

What was that all about?

Israel and the Arab states have hated each other ever since Israel became a nation in 1948. The Arab states lost that first war. Hundreds of thousands of Palestinian refugees found themselves without a homeland, and none of the other Arab states wanted them. In 1956, they lost the second major conflict when England, France, and Israel took the Suez Canal back from Egyptian President Nasser, when he tried to nationalize it.

Early in 1967, Syrian-backed Palestinian guerrillas began attacks across the Israeli border, and Israel retaliated. In April, 1967, Israel and Syria duked it out with artillery and in the air, and Syria lost six fighter jets. Humiliating.

The Soviet Union gave Egypt the information that Israel was moving troops to their northern border for a full-scale invasion of Syria. It was not true, but Nasser bought it. He sent troops into the Sinai Peninsula. These troops kicked out a United Nations peacekeeping force that had been there for ten years. The Egyptians had allowed the UN to keep the peace until a better opportunity presented itself for the Egyptians to attack Israel. The situation deteriorated further, and Israel finally decided to launch a preemptive attack.

On June 5, 1967, Israel sent some 200 aircraft toward Egypt from the north. They caught the Egyptians by surprise and attacked 18 different airfields, eliminating about 90 percent of the Egyptian air force on the ground. Israel then turned north and decimated all the air forces of Jordan, Syria, and Iraq. All in one day.

With full control of the skies, Israel took the ground war into the Sinai Peninsula and the Gaza Strip. When Egypt ordered a retreat, complete confusion consumed the Egyptian forces and Israel pushed the routed Egyptians all the way across the Sinai.

Jordon had heard that Egypt had won the war and began shelling Israeli positions in Jerusalem. Israel responded with devastating accuracy against East Jerusalem and the West Bank.

On June 7, Israeli troops took the Old City of Jerusalem.

Syria had heavily fortified the Golan Heights, but on June 9-10, Israeli tanks and infantry captured the city of Golan.

On June 10, the UN declared a cease-fire. They probably didn't want Israel to take the entire Middle East. Six days, 20,000 Arabs and 800 Israeli died in 132 hours of fighting.

Somewhere at the beginning or in the middle of that Six Day War, President Lyndon Johnson had committed two complete airborne divisions to defend Israel from the Arab world. While our 101st Airborne Division was still on the runway, the 82nd Airborne Division had already lifted off and was circling the airfield waiting for the President's order to fly to Israel. Israel won that war so quickly, that they didn't need our help.

I've never been to Israel or the Middle East yet, but I'm glad that my first encounter was not in combat. I've always wondered what my life would have been like if my first trip overseas had been a firefight in the middle of the Egyptian desert. Assuming I had survived it.

While that near-combat experience was limited to sitting on a plane, our next mission taught us live crowd control with loaded weapons and unsheathed bayonets.

In Detroit, Michigan, at 3:30 a.m., on Sunday, July 23, the police had raided a raucous after-hours drinking and gambling club (a "blind pic") at 12ᵗʰ and Clairmount. The riot ignited immediately. Looting and arson swept through the early morning and afternoon hours, as Detroit police rejected the use of tear gas and firearms in their attempt to bring the riot under control. The officials ordered the policemen to passively stop the riot (no arrests) in the 12th Street area, where several thousand people had joined the riot.

That approach failed miserably. By 3 p.m. Sunday, the riot had spread west to Linwood Avenue and the Governor mobilized the National Guard. Initially, city officials managed to keep the local media from reporting on the swelling disorder, but rumors and fires sparked radio and TV reports that afternoon. By dusk on Sunday, the riots had spread in all directions, and Mayor Jerome Cavanagh ordered the closing of all bars, theaters, and gas stations. All the rioters ignored a 9 p.m. curfew.

On Monday morning, July 24, the riot escalated even further. The rioters had resorted to placing snipers on rooftops. From upstairs windows, they pinned down police officers on four streets. By late afternoon, thirty fires burned out of control, while snipers and looters fought with the police and fire fighters.

Cavanagh finally requested military intervention to support the local law enforcement in reestablishing law and order. President Johnson sent in the 101st Airborne Division. Our unit pacified the east side of town, while the National Guard struggled on the west side.

Rumors ran rampant, and everybody was quick to express his own version of the causes. In our airborne company we had whites and Afro-Americans, and I never sensed any racial tension between anyone in our units.

Somehow, we had been trained to view the enemy as the person shooting *at* you, not the guy standing next to you shooting back, regardless of his skin color. In any case, we weren't in a position to philosophize. We had a bigger problem.

Obviously, as common soldiers, we knew nothing about what was going on at that time. We thought that we had been sent there to stop the riots. But what was the function of the military in a hometown scenario? We all knew that the police were tasked to protect the people from violence, and that the National Guard were trained to protect the country from outside invaders. These two powers defended people. The military, on the other hand, kills the enemy. Everything about our training screamed: Kill the enemy! We were an attack-trained team of Airborne soldiers sent to support defensive-trained units of police and national guard.

So were the crowds the enemy? We weren't the police. We weren't going to arrest anyone. We weren't the National Guard. We weren't fighting invaders. What were we seriously supposed to do?

That was easy. Follow orders.

When we arrived in Detroit, the drills in crowd control commenced immediately. A point man took the lead of a V-shaped formation with two men directly behind him. The men in the left line placed their right front shoulders firmly against the left rear shoulder of the man in front of them. The men in the right line placed their left front shoulders firmly against the right rear shoulder of the man in front of them. The V-shape formed a wedge. The wedge moved forward thrusting ten fixed bayonets on ten rifles and everyone yelling, "Hup! Hup! Hup!" in unison. The formation and yelling was intended to scare and disperse a crowd of rioters who didn't want to be skewered by our wedge of bayonets. I don't think any of us believed that we were actually going to charge into a crowd of rioters stabbing bodies, flinging them off to the side like hot dogs, while keeping our formation intact, and continuing to stab the next person in front of us who was stupid enough to get in our way.

One soldier told us that he felt weird being on the other end of the riot. When we asked him what he meant, he admitted to having taken part in the Watts Riots in California in August, 1965. He had been on the roof tops throwing rocks down on the police. Then he got drafted, and now he was on the receiving end. We didn't discuss his motivations for his part in the Watts Riots.

We never ran into a crowd. We were ordered to clear both sides of a street once, i.e., stop any more looting, etc., but all we found were destroyed businesses.

We were more concerned about the nerves of the National Guard personnel. They weren't facing the enemy. What if they really were ordered to shoot somebody who turned out to be a neighbor? Their taut nerves worried us. We wondered if we shouldn't offer to hold their weapons for them, so they didn't accidentally shoot someone, like us. Dozens of cigarette butts littered the ground around the wheels of a jeep where a National Guardsman sat behind a 50-calibre machine-gun.

A 50-calibre carries a lot of punch. As a sniper rifle, it was built to take down a hovering helicopter, penetrate armored vehicles, and blow up bulk fuel tanks over a mile away. A single trained marksman could take out a target over 1,800 yards away. The 50-calibre 82A1 was light enough to be carried by one person and the muzzle break reduced the kick to that of a 12-gauge shotgun. The man sitting behind that 50-calibre became a sniper's primary target.

Looking toward the tall buildings directly in front of him, he kept his darting and frantic eyes glued to their rooftops looking for snipers. One rumor surfaced that when another guardsman stumbled getting out of a jeep, he used the butt of his rifle to stop his fall. He had, however, left the safety off, and his weapon fired. The guardsman behind the 50-caliber lit up the rooftops with a couple hundred rounds of ammo before an officer, whose screams could not be heard over the explosions of 10 rounds per second, jumped in the jeep and stopped him.

Our unit never received the command to skewer someone with our bayonets or shoot someone. Once the riots were over, we stayed a couple days longer to let everyone know that we were still there, ready and willing to skewer, but we were allowed to become tourists for one day. I visited an outdoor naval museum and spent half the day inside a World War II submarine. Tight quarters. I was glad that I had chosen to jump out of airplanes.

We returned to the boring life of the base. I wrote to Mom to calm her fears when she heard the news that my unit had spent some time in Detroit. I might want to brag to the ladies about how much we had not done there, but with Mom I wrote a lot about the inside of a submarine.

Wayne and I hung out at the PX, the food store and bar on base. In order to stay away from any officers wanting to exercise their authority by having us pick up cigarette butts on the parade ground, Wayne and I exchanged dollars for nickels so we could play the two pinball machines all day long. Officers rarely entered that PX.

Toward evening on one of those days, six drunk Afro-American soldiers wanted to start a fight. Wayne and I tried to leave, but they cornered us just outside. Wayne's first two punches dropped two of them cold. That left two on him and two on me. One of my attackers came up with a knife. I managed to deck him just as he got close enough to leave me with a small permanent scar under my chin. His buddy ran off. Before the other two could attack Wayne again, another Afro-American soldier, who had been in our unit earlier, came to Wayne's defense by throwing himself through the air and body slamming one of Wayne's attackers onto the ground. The battle was over.

News of our skirmish was all over the barracks when we returned. If I remember correctly, our Platoon leader, Lieutenant Pershing, was the great grandson of the General Pershing in World War I. Lieutenant Pershing asked me what the other guy looked like. The knife wound wasn't deep, but my blood soaked my entire shirt and part of my pants. The lieutenant told me to clean up and meet with him and the captain to give our side of the incident.

When, Jeremiah, my Afro-American M60 gunner found out about the fight, he wanted to defend his squad leader. As mentioned earlier, we had very little racism in our unit. Jeremiah was built like Godzilla's cousin. Nobody messed with Jeremiah. His assistant gunner, Johnson, looked like a dwarf next to Jeremiah. I think they enlisted together as close friends and managed to stay together all the way through Basic Training, Advanced Infantry Training, Jump School, and ended up in Vietnam in the same platoon with Wayne and myself.

Eventually, the soldier who tried to stab me got arrested in Vietnam for a number of crimes. My testimony was useless, because the fight took place in the evening, and I couldn't clearly identify him. Even so, he no longer looked confident and arrogant. If convicted, he would face at least a year in prison in Vietnam, and then either have to serve out the rest of his time in Vietnam or be dishonorably discharged. The military court found him guilty on the evidence of other testimonies.

Boredom was finally replaced with the anticipation of the rumors that our unit was on levy for Vietnam. In September semi-orders replaced the rumors. Platoon leaders announced that everyone should take off and use up as much leave time as they had saved up. Wayne went home and came back a married man. I wasn't jealous. I just wondered why someone would get married right before being sent to Vietnam as a combat soldier?

I wrote to Mom. I don't remember how much I got paid each month, but the Army wanted to know how much of our monthly pay we wanted to receive in the field while we were in Vietnam. I realized that I would need very little money in combat, so I requested $20 a month, and I asked that the rest be sent home to Mom. She could spend it as she liked, or save it for me, or whatever.

We shipped out December 15, 1967. My almost-combat experience in the Middle East and Detroit was about to become the real thing.

3. DECEMBER, 1967: ENTERING ENEMY TERRITORY

We landed on Wake Island on the flight to Vietnam. A coral atoll with a 12-mile coastline rising just above sea level forms that island roughly 2,300 miles west of Hawaii and 2,000 miles east of Tokyo. During World War II, the US Marines fought off the first wave of Japanese soldiers for the island on December 11, 1941, but the Japanese overpowered them during the second attack on December 23rd.

Remoteness describes a location that requires more than effort to reach. Isolation describes a location that few people ever reach. Surrounded by 360-degrees of undrinkable salt water, Wake Island is the epitome of isolation. The Marshall Islands, their nearest neighbors, poke their heads out of the blue bathtub 592 miles southeast. Wake serves as a mid-Pacific refueling stop for military aircraft and emergency landings. The longest runway in the Pacific Islands, 9,800 feet, transforms the sand and sharp coral into a welcome mat for exhausted aviators during their long, tedious, and boring flights across an expanse so large, that even from 30,000 feet in the air, only a blue horizon fills their vision. Today the Ronald Reagan Ballistic Missile Defense Test Site calls Wake Island its home. Less than 100 people live on the island, and access is restricted. No permanent residents. Not for tourists. The residents rely partially on "rainwater catchments" for their drinking water.

We spent the night and slept in huge hangars of some kind. We asked what it was like to be stationed on Wake Island. One second lieutenant had bought a new car and had it shipped to Wake Island. The salt had corroded through the entire vehicle in less than eight months.

We landed somewhere in our new home, Vietnam, and they packed us into trucks and transported us to our base at Bien Hoa located in South-Central Vietnam about 16 miles from Saigon, across the Dong Nam river. As we drove across a bridge, I snuck out my small pocket camera and snapped three pictures. Lush forests on both sides of a river ran into the distance and the bridge railing blocked my attempt at a perfect picture. Astronomical amounts of Agent Orange toxins have penetrated the air base since the end of the war. The base was scheduled to begin cleanup by 2019.

The humidity struck. Hot and muggy and insects. If I hadn't wished for a shotgun to shoot the mosquitos, I could have become an entomophile (insect lover). Because our unit's Search and Destroy missions took us all over the place, we spent little time at our main base camp. I never remembered the names of all the locations we stayed in between missions. Large tents with cots and mosquito netting. Mess hall and latrines. No luxuries, just survival needs.

I'm not writing a strict chronology of all our missions. Most resulted in no contact with enemy. Those were the times when war didn't seem so bad and some funny things happened. Those missions that resulted in combat were all the same, in many ways. If the enemy attacked us, we had no time to be afraid. We did what we were trained to do. Most soldiers will understand the previous two sentences. If we attacked the enemy, then it was either through a planned ambush or we surprised each other and, a fire fight took place. Many ambushes turned out to be eight hours of sitting quietly in our formation, having no enemy walk into it, getting up and going back to the base. If an enemy unit did stumble into one of our jungle traps, we all clicked the button labeled "fight mode" in our brains and did our jobs. I will only describe those missions or patrols that made the largest impact on me emotionally. Fifty years have erased some of the exact timing between missions and things that happened between the missions.

It should be obvious that a lower E-4 enlisted person like myself was never informed as to the larger picture. We followed orders, went where we were told to go, shot or blew up the enemy, and returned to base camp when the fire fights were over.

An E-5 sergeant (three rockers/stripes) usually led a squad, but when I arrived, they had lost too many E-5s, so even though I was still an E-4, I functioned as a squad leader.

Our platoon had two M60 machine gunner teams. Two guys formed one M60 team with one gunner and one assistant gunner. Randal was short and not at all muscular, but he loved his M60. I think he viewed it as an item of prestige being able to carry a weapon that dwarfed him. He did his job well, but he was a bit foolish at times. We needed to cross a stream once, and without thinking, he decided to be the first one to see how deep it was. Carrying his pack in addition to his 23- pound weapon, fully loaded with a belt of 7.62 rounds, he stepped into the creek and immediately disappeared out of sight. The two guys behind him ditched their gear, sprang in behind him and pulled him out, gear and all. Cuss words flowed from the guys who pulled him out, but Randal looked so much like a drowned rat, that if the enemy had attacked us at that time, we would have all died laughing.

I've already mentioned the other M60 team, Jeremiah and Johnson. Jeremiah's body bulged with muscles of a small giant. Johnson, his assistant, could have been blown away by a breeze. His equipment held him on the ground. We wondered how he could walk at all. He had to carry his own pack as well as a couple extra boxes of ammunition, 1,500 rounds in each box, and an extra M60 barrel. If the gunner fired too many rounds instead of short bursts, he would melt the barrel. Once a round pierced the top of the barrel, the groves in the barrel no longer guided the rounds in the right direction, and they went in every direction.

BETWEEN PATROLS

Between missions, we were always trying to increase our comfort. Or at least the officers gave jobs to the enlisted men to increase the comfort of the officers.

Staying clean seldom happened. The officers got to take

showers, while we washed out of our helmets. We joked about the officers needing the showers more than the enlisted men. We tried, but usually failed, to avoid being tasked to help the officers stay clean(er).

I received the assignment to join a sergeant and two privates in building a shower for the officers. The sergeant would give me an order, and I would pass the order along to one of the privates. The end result would provide the officers with a high wooden tower with a 55-gallon drum on top. A generator would pump water into that drum, and the officers would stand under it to take their showers.

Somebody else had already built the tower. The four of us needed to convert the gasoline drum into a water drum. Those drums have very small holes in one end. We struggled to lift the drum in the air and empty all the fuel out of it before it could be used as a water container for a shower. Oil and water falling all over your body only appealed to us if a naked officer was under the shower.

As we pondered our dilemma, one of the privates stood off to the side of the barrel, while another private stood directly in front the barrel's small opening. I stood 10-15 feet away facing the barrel. The sergeant had a brilliant idea. Giving no thought to the repercussions of his solution, he stepped up to the side of the hole and struck a match. The soldier in front of the barrel had no time to react. I had about three seconds. I turned and attempted to sprint in the opposite direction. The flame touched the hole and the explosion lifted the soldier into the air and threw him some distance away. He hit the ground unhurt. Apparently, he had been so close to the blast, that the air pressure apparently protected him from the flames that followed the initial burst. The sergeant wasn't hurt. He had not been in the line of the blast.

I jumped away from the flames, but not quickly enough. The flame targeted my lower body, which motivated my legs to propel my backside forward in a frantic attempt to avoid being roasted like what we had just eaten for lunch in the mess hall. My arms acted like rear guards that had stationed themselves between the enemy and safety. They pushed away from the flames and propelled my body forward in their futile attempt to shield the rest of my body from the flames. My arms took the brunt of the burns.

I had not fallen down, but the medics strapped me onto the stretcher, wheeled me into an ambulance and deposited me at the field hospital a few minutes away. It was just bad luck that the nurses had a lull in their number of patients. The head nurse made use of her rank to take my case. She treated me for second-degree burns on my arms and my bottom. Yes, the burns hurt, but I was more distressed by the fact that all the hospital personnel were nurses. They crowded into my room to watch while the head nurse had me disrobe completely, while facing her and the nurses, and then lay down on a cot, while she treated the burns on my bottom. In war time, you take thrills wherever you can get them.

The sergeant who lit us up that day was transferred immediately to another unit. I don't know if he kept his rank. A new mission came along, and I don't think the officers got their shower. I didn't even get a Purple Heart for my first wounds in Vietnam.

I still have a couple pictures of myself digging a large trench at that base camp with both my arms bandaged up. I was holding a cigarette in my mouth, a beer in one hand, and a shovel in the other. I knew Mom would laugh at that picture, since she knew that I didn't smoke or drink. I'm not anti-alcohol. I had just already seen too much damage done to other people by both of those activities.

Mom sent me some packs of Koolaid® powder. The humid and hot weather drained us on the missions. The mess sergeant had trouble keeping enough ice on hand for the officers. Whenever we returned from a mission, one of our squad members would find the mess sergeant and talk to him about whatever, in order to get him away from the ice cooler. Another squad member would find the ice cooler (the sergeant kept moving it around), fill his metal helmet with as much ice as possible and bring it to me. I would pour the

Koolaid® all over the ice in the helmet. Then our squad would drink the liquid and suck on the Koolaid® covered chunks of ice that hadn't melted yet. One accepts comforts where one can find such comforts.

C-RATIONS

The C-Rations were tolerable. The "lifers," soldiers who had been in the army since Rome fell, informed us that the K-Rations during World War II were the equivalent of dog food. C-Rations eaten cold would choke the strongest veteran.

One retired officer called the contents of those green cans of C-Rations the equivalent of shoe leather, if they were heated up. At least they were portable and didn't seem to spoil. If they had spoiled, we might not have known the difference. One meal contained 2,990 calories with sufficient vitamins to keep a man alive long enough to engage the enemy. Twelve different menus, each with one canned meat item, one canned fruit or bread or dessert item, one "B unit" of crackers or chocolate, and an accessory packet of cigarettes, matches, chewing gum, toilet paper, coffee, creamer, sugar, and salt. Oh, and a spoon. If a chopper accidentally dropped a box of C-Rations from the air, they usually were still edible.

Different GIs liked different things in the C-Ration packages. For some reason our unit like the canned peaches the best. Maybe because that's what we ended up getting every time we opened our package.

We called the chopped ham and eggs "H.E.s" (high explosives) because they caused bloating and gas.

We used "heat tabs" to warm up the C-Rations. We couldn't use them inside a closed shelter due to the terrible fumes.

Nobody liked the Ham and Lima Beans. Nobody. Loathing is the best description for that so-called food. Those cans were called the "ham and mo-fo's." I won't translate the meaning of that term.

Some GIs tried to improve the taste by dousing them with hot sauce or steak sauce. It was a waste of the sauce. One story surfaced that some soldiers tried to heat the cans by strapping them to the engine mufflers of their vehicles. They forgot to punch holes in the cans to release the steam. The explosion would have shamed C-Company's mortar barrage, and the stench lasted for days.

Some guys used C-4, the explosive, to warm up their food. They said that a small chunk burned like Sterno, but you should never stomp on it to put it out. I never tried C-4.

The P-38 can opener worked all the time. It never jammed, like some of our M16s. It could also function as a knife to pry open anything, including field strip a soldier's weapon. Even dig out an ingrown toenail. Practical. I held onto my P-38 for years.

I made a fortune from the cigarettes in the C-Rations. I didn't smoke, but I found out who did. If I remember correctly, four cigarettes came with every package of C-Rations. The heavy smokers smoked their way out of cigarettes early during the week. I was ready to trade. Pall Mall, Luckies, Winston, Salem and Benson & Hedges Menthol. I loved the peaches, but I traded them early in the week for cigarettes. My pocketbook took priority over my taste buds.

On one of our patrols, I saw our point man take a hit in the back as the attack started. We saw him arch his back as he fell forward. When the firefight was over, and we reached his position, he was sitting up, rubbing his back, and going through his backpack. When he pulled his hand out of his backpack, his hand was all sticky. The first thought was that it was his blood, but it wasn't the right color. It was a clear liquid. In his hand he held a gooey can of peaches.

"Why my peaches!?" he screamed.

His entire backpack was drenched in wet peach juice. At that point, he raised the gooey can of peaches into the air and began cussing and yelling, "Why couldn't he have hit my ham and lima beans!"

I don't know why that bullet didn't penetrate any further

than inside his can of peaches.

At one point, we got so tired of C-Rations, that one of the guys threw a grenade into a pond. After the explosion, he dove in and began throwing dead fish onto the grass. We had lots of fish for our next couple of meals.

The Long Range Recon Patrols, aka "LRRPs" (pronounced "lurps"), got much better meals than anyone else. These food packets, "LRP rations" (also pronounced "lurp"), were a luxury. Man-sized meals, freeze-dried in plastic bags, lighter than C-Rations, ideal for long missions. Most important, they tasted much better. Yes, frozen dinners from Safeway were luxury meals. When these "lurps" came through the rear-echelon troops, only four of the original 20 meals reached the LRRP guys.

MOVIES

To keep the troops from going stir-crazy between firefights, our office personnel received permission to show movies outdoors. A make-shift screen, a reel projector and an old comedy. No rain, yet.

During one of those movies, and with just thirty minutes left of the movie, two soldiers wanted a beer. The bar was still open. They tossed for it; one lost, jumped up and ran off. To relax he had taken off his boots. He left them by his chair. A couple minutes later the mortars arrived. The reel man took a vote. Stop the movie and head for cover or continue watching. Almost unanimous. Continue watching. None of the mortars came close to the movie area. One landed on the opposite side of the bar.

The guy with the beers? He had run back, barefoot, unharmed, without spilling a drop. When he sat down, he asked, "What did I miss?" He wasn't referring to the mortars.

LIEUTENANTS

Lieutenants in Vietnam usually received three months of

training at Officer Candidate School. It seemed like they spent most of their time in that school learning from books and keeping their rooms spotlessly clean. They were seriously undertrained for combat, or for leadership in general. Years later, I learned that the average age of a second lieutenant during World War II was 26 years old. In Vietnam, he was 19. Boys. We relied on the upper-level Non-Commissioned Officers (E-6 and higher), who had survived more than a few months, to keep us alive. On smaller missions, anyone over 21 with four months of combat experience commanded the unit, regardless of who gave the commands.

Another mission. In the north, somewhere. We enlisted men seldom had access to a map. I was selling cigarettes when the mortars came in. We sat between two forest-covered hills. I was raised in Colorado. Colorado has mountains. Everybody else has hills. The enemy had placed their mortars on the side of the hill we could see. We loved it when the enemy made it convenient to engage them. Even between the deep foliage, the sun's rays bounced off their equipment. Our artillery responded with deadly accuracy. Only lasted a few minutes. A new second lieutenant thought we all needed more to do, so he ordered us to start cleaning up the area. He was practicing his new position of power.

"Yes, Sir!" We looked busy and then ignored him when he left. In broad daylight, he put one soldier on watch. No one was sleeping. The enemy rarely attacked in the open. This was jungle warfare. We would know the enemy was near by the mortar fire or a sniper round whizzing past our heads. We never "saw" the enemy. A few minutes later the lieutenant caught that soldier sitting on the ground, leaning against something with his eyes closed. The lieutenant threatened to have him busted down a rank. Never happened. The lieutenant and his small unit of a few men never returned from their next recon mission.

Army Regulations prohibited a soldier from bringing his own weapon to Vietnam, but some guys did anyway. One guy had a small .22 pistol. After some new lieutenant had needlessly gotten an enlisted man killed, someone suggested that we should shoot the lieutenant in the leg with the .22 to get him out of there. That got bantered around awhile, until someone finally pointed out that the doctor would recognize a .22 hole over an enemy weapon, that the person who did it would have to do it so it looked like the enemy did it, and that the lieutenant would get a Purple Heart for bravery in action. We all rolled our eyes and geared up for our next patrol.

4. DECEMBER, 1967 – FEBRUARY 5, 1968: PATROLS

FIRST PATROL

On December 25, 1967, we began our first patrol as a training exercise to acclimatize us to the area. It ended in a full-scale firefight. The day before we had been guaranteed a hot meal for Christmas. Our mess hall could accommodate our entire unit. Did I say guaranteed? The cooks handed out heat tablets for our C-Rations because we were heading out on our first mission.

We began by scouting out an area that was reported "secure." We came to distrust all such designations. It remained secure for about twenty minutes, then all hell broke loose. We found ourselves in a full-scale battle. The enemy might have opened fire too soon, because we automatically deployed (spread out) and returned fire without taking heavy losses.

Our point man turned 21 that day. He died that day. He was the first of our unit to die in combat. An ironic Christmas present. I didn't see him fall. I only saw the body after it was all over.

We fanned out, dropped to the ground, and low-crawled while returning fire toward the enemy's location. We determined the enemy's location by the noise of his weapons. Not very accurate, since a firefight is all noise. The jungle made it impossible to see the enemy. A fire fight usually lasted just a few minutes, but larger units usually took more time to stop killing each other. We (enlisted men) were seldom told how many of the enemy we had killed. We just counted our own dead.

We had called in a Huey, a helicopter. After the pilot had unloaded his arsenal, the enemy got lucky and struck him with a rocket. The Huey did not explode and disintegrate, but it had no hope of landing properly. We saw the pilot, knowing that he was going to die, steer his machine down on top of the enemy position. We received no more enemy fire from that position after the explosion.

I've had lots of thoughts that have come and gone over the last fifty-two years since my time in Nam, but the thought has never left me: that soldier's and that pilot's relatives back home on the day after Christmas. I still choke up thinking about the pain that evil causes. It's just not right that a life should be snuffed out so early, so young, with so much future, and the collateral damage done to those who hoped to share in that life. I thought mostly about those who did not look to Jesus for support in those times. How sad that they have no answers for their questions about evil, no gaining of God's support as they process through their pain and loss. I prayed that God would draw really, really close to Mom if God chose to end my life in Nam. I knew, deep down inside, that God, who knows all, but allows evil, makes everything work out perfectly for those who love Him. And I knew that Mom loved Jesus.

CHARLIE COMPANY

I never met any of the guys who served in the Charlie Company in our unit. They had the reputation of begin drunk all the time, but when we needed some mortars dropped on the enemy, even in the middle of the night, their accuracy was so perfect, that we began to wonder if they weren't angelic beings who hadn't been so angelic in heaven and had to serve a time of penance in a human war.

Radio training drilled the radio codes into our radiomen. If we needed a barrage of mortars, Charlie Company usually didn't need a trial run with correction for the second volley. If their first round hit the target, the radioman would say, "Fire for effect," and the earth hiccuped as the mortars rained terror.

I don't know if the terms are correct, but another unit experienced a new radioman who, under fire, mixed up his terms. The officer told him to call in a barrage of mortars.

That worked fine, and the unit moved into the enemy's position where the mortars had dropped. The radioman heard a message from Charlie Company, probably something like, "Satisfied with our delivery?" The radioman hadn't been ready for that message, did not understand it, and replied, "Repeat that." The officer grabbed the radio handset and screamed into it, "Belay that! Belay that!" The radioman should have said, "Say again." "Repeat" meant that Charlie Company was to send some more mortars onto the same position as previously fired upon.

MORE PATROLS

I saw my first dead enemy on a patrol. He was lying on his back. An M16 round had entered the front of this head. The man in front of me turned him over with his boot. The entire back of this head had been evaporated.

I learned to be very quiet on patrols. I watched where I stepped while looking in all directions at the same time. Yes, I needed to care about the men in my squad, but if I died, I couldn't help them anyway. Stories abound of soldiers dying to save another soldier. That happened a lot, but if a sergeant got killed, everyone else got nervous. When a lieutenant got killed, we knew we could trust the sergeant. I didn't want to become a sergeant. Too many people would end up depending on me. I just wanted to go home.

I began praying for rain on patrols. Nobody thought that we were going to end this war by winning it. That would only happen if we nuked Hanoi and then asked the Chinese or Russians what they were going to do about it. The point was nothing more than to survive the year and go home.

In my experience, which was not everyone's experience, there were fewer attacks in the rain on patrols. Yes, I knew it was possible to initiate, or be on the receiving end of, an attack in the rain. Others had killed and died in attacks during the rainy season. But for me, I couldn't see as far in the rain. Sound became my best friend and protector. I made my peace with the rain. I still love it when it rains. I could use a bunch of adjectives and adverbs to describe the rain, but for me, the most vivid recollection are two things: softly quiet and less death.

One day we snuggled up on a hill next to a bunch of Marines. We noticed that they were using M14s instead of M16s. The conversation went something like this.

"The M14 isn't a jungle weapon. Too heavy. And the ammunition is too heavy and bulky. Why are you using it? The M16 and ammo are so much lighter."

The marine smirked. "The M14 always works. Deadly accurate. The M16 jams a lot."

"Ah, here let me show you how to solve that problem." I picked up an M16 and showed them the small plastic rectangular tube of oil taped on the stock just in front of the chamber when the round entered. "The M16 doesn't have any kind of cleaning mechanism to get rid of the carbon formed in the chamber when a round is fired. If the carbon cools just a little, it gets hard, and then the bolt can't move forward all the way to engage the next round." I held up the weapon with my left hand, with my fingers on the tube of oil and gently squeezed. "During a firefight, you just keep squeezing this tube all the time. A firefight seldom lasts long enough to empty the tube. Then, if you're still alive, refill the tube for the next time."

The next day some of the Marines had taken back their M16s. They gave us some of their food. I remember liking the change from our C-Rations. They were probably C-Rations, too, but I never noticed.

The stock of the M14 was heavy wood. You could knock someone out with the butt of the M14. The M16 was made from plastic. During a very short firefight, my M16 failed to fire properly on automatic. When I fired it, it didn't chamber the next round. I looked at the chamber. No carbon stopping the next round from entering the chamber. I manually chambered the next round and fired. One round went down range. It hadn't chambered the next round. I had to keep manually loading the next round. I was lucky enough to have made it through that skirmish without automatic fire.

When it was over, I checked the entire weapon and found a very thin crack in the stock. A small amount of dirt had entered the stock of the weapon and hindered the bolt from retracting back far enough to allow the next round to enter the slot before the chamber. The bolt simply slid over the next round. The lieutenant procured a new M16 for me.

We were on that hill with those Marines for a couple of days and nights. We had been moving lots with very little sleep. We caught naps when we could. We were never told where we were going next, only that we had be ready to move at any time. I felt like we were chasing some fugitives.

We dug our fox holes on the top slope of a hill surrounded by forest. The high ground should have given us the advantage, but the jungle wiped out that advantage. We didn't know where the enemy was, but they could see our position for miles.

They attacked us two nights in a row. They snuck up the ridge and tossed grenades toward our fox holes. We had dug decoy fox holes further down the ridge. The Vietcong made them deeper with their grenades. We had no casualties.

Lieutenant Pershing sent me and three guys down the slope just after nightfall to see if we could hear where the enemy was coming from. Each of us had two hours to stay awake to discover the enemy's approach. I told the guys to wake me up if they heard even the snap of a twig. I was more worried about the enemy getting so close that they would hear our radio when we called in their presence. Why couldn't we fight this war with quieter radios?

The enemy did attack our lines that night, but the four of us had all fallen asleep. Considering our lack of sleep, I think it would have been impossible to stay awake.

The next morning, we called in from down the ridge to ask when we should return. The lieutenant had already sent out a squad to find out what had happened to us. He thought we had been wiped out. We truthfully claimed that we never heard them go by. None of our men had been killed in the attack that night. The enemy obviously didn't know we were there, or they would have silently killed us. I think that the lieutenant had trouble believing our story, but since the enemy could have moved past us during anyone's watch, no one admitted to falling asleep. The lieutenant decided to not send any more recon units out. If we had stayed awake, I'm not sure we could have heard the enemy anyway. They knew how to be silent in the jungle better than we did.

The next night, I took a forward position in a shallow foxhole about 50 feet down the hill in front of my squad. Not as far forward as the previous night, but I really wanted to try and hear the enemy crawling up the hill. Maybe I felt bad about falling asleep the night before. I fell asleep again.

I suddenly felt someone shaking my shoulder. I woke up mad. I was dead tired, and it had better be the lieutenant who was waking me up and not some private. Then I heard the voice of one of my squad members.

"Sarge, you need to get out of this hole. The Vietcong are walking the mortars straight up this hill, and you've going to take a direct hit." He wasn't the apocalyptic type who screamed, "We're all gonna die!" So I crawled out of the foxhole up the ridge to the next one. I rolled into it with two other guys just as a mortar round deepened my previous location by five feet. I gave that soldier my entire rations for the week. I lost twenty pounds during my tour in Vietnam.

TACTICS

If the enemy lured us into a trap during a mission, our survival depended on killing the enemy before his surprise succeeded. We charged toward the enemy and engaged the enemy directly. A trap attempts to drive the surprised soldiers away from the initial fire of the enemy and into the fire of more well-placed enemy fire and mines, which finished the battle with little damage to the attackers. If we went toward the enemy, we had a fifty-fifty chance of surviving. If we went in any other direction, death was guaranteed. When I turned toward the gun fire, my squad turned toward the gun fire. Obviously, I never got killed.

In 2003, I went to see the movie, *Tears of the Sun*, with my two sons and a few of my college students. In that movie, Bruce Willis leads a band of soldiers into enemy territory to save some innocent people from a local war. In the process, his band is ambushed. The team immediately turns toward the enemy and returns fire. During that scene, past images resurrected in my mind. I don't know if I showed anything to the others through my body language, but when the movie ended, both my sons asked me if I was all right. I said yes, and that I would see them tomorrow. Right after they left, I bought a movie ticket to watch a Disney film that was playing afterwards. I didn't want the images from Vietnam to be the last thing in my mind before I went to sleep. I don't remember the Disney movie.

Some of the Nam visions have since become fuzzy. War movies playing on the screen are great if you have never really experienced the fear and death and horror of having lost a comrade in war. Time and memory loss can be a wonderful healer.

Some guys wanted the action of combat. A few believed in what we were doing over there. If they got wounded, those men came back for a second or third tour. Others stated openly that there was no honor in this war. We weren't saving anybody from anyone. The philosophy behind the war was the West's fight against Communism. The philosophy in the field was to become a "short-timer" as quickly as possible. No one knew how to make time go faster but waking up in the morning meant that you had made it through another day. Seeing an empty bunk reminded you that your bunk might be empty tomorrow morning.

I've seldom watched Vietnam movies since my time in Nam. Years later, my family and I were visiting an American Air Force captain and his family in London. He was working in military intelligence and was surrounded by Brits. They kept asking him about Vietnam. He kept pointing out that he was too young to have served in Vietnam.

My friend invited me to go see the movie, *Platoon*, and tell him how realistic the movie was. I refused to go, but he bribed me with a lobster dinner in a posh restaurant in downtown London. I should have hated the movie, but I didn't. The emotions had ceased to plague me. I informed my friend that, from my perspective, the film was quite realistic. The lobster dinner was excellent.

A few infantry guys, like myself, made it through their twelve months unscathed. Numerous patrols produced nothing more than lots of exercise. No one died on those patrols. Then the rumors began circulating that a number of units were going to move out at the same time. This was a mission, not an isolated search and destroy patrol.

5. FEBRUARY 5, 1968: WOUNDED

We seldom spent time in our home base camp of Bien Hoa. I lost track of how many other base camps we dropped into for the next Search and Destroy patrol.

At one of those base camps, I met a soldier who was so near-sighted, that he couldn't see the sights on the end of his M16 barrel. A slight exaggeration, but not much. His MOS (title for his job description) was 11B, a grunt, a ground soldier. He hadn't been in a firefight yet, but it was obvious that his first encounter with enemy would send him home early in a body-bag.

A clerk position opened up in our unit, and for some reason, probably because I could type well, one of my superiors offered it to me. I don't know why I didn't take it. Had I asked anyone with a brain for advice, they would have informed me that I had joined the insane for turning it down. Maybe I still wanted to see more combat. What a pathetic human being!

When is enough enough? No one believed that we were there to right some wrongs. Only a few gung-ho higher-ups were preaching honor and glory. Most were preaching body count. The rest of us were just following orders.

I don't remember how that soldier and I connected, but I offered him the clerk job. He almost cried. He accepted my offer. His reaction told me that he was eternally grateful for my gift.

An E-5 promotion had opened up, and I was second on the list to receive it. The man ahead of me had a good reputation as a good leader. He knew how to take care of himself and his men in the field. A couple of nights before the promotion became official, he got drunk, got into a small fight, and got caught. The officer in charge had no alternative but to bust him down to E-3.

The lieutenant informed me that I would be receiving the

promotion. The now E-3 took it really hard. He didn't hate me, but we couldn't look each other in the eye. He had earned the promotion. He deserved it. He screwed up. Bitterness oozed through his response: "Shit happens."

Before I could receive the promotion, however, the rumors of a major mission materialized, and a number of companies geared up to move out. Something was happening. Per Lieutenant Pershing's order, I was given official command of a squad with Jeremiah and Johnson as my M60 gunner team. I was still an E-4 squad leader.

It was February 4, 1968.

The Vietnamese New Year, the first day of spring and the most important national holiday in Vietnam, fell on January 30, 1968, celebrating the Lunar New Year. "Tet" is short for "thank goodness!" meaning that a new year has arrived, and everyone can start all over.

In previous years, both North and South Vietnam had agreed to an informal truce in the Vietnam war on this holiday. In early 1968, however, the North Vietnamese military commander, General Vo Nguyen Giap, chose January 31 to carry out coordinated surprise attacks by the North Vietnamese on more than 100 cities and outposts in South Vietnam. Giap's goal was to cause the Army of the Republic of Vietnam (ARVN) forces to collapse and to motivate the South Vietnamese population to rebel. He also believed that this offensive would drive a wedge between the Americans and the South Vietnamese. Some sources state that America lost a couple hundred men, while the North Vietnamese lost over 5,000. The American Media, however, convinced the American public that America was losing the War in Vietnam, and America chose to pull out.

Lieutenant Pershing might have been informed about the beginning of the Tet Offensive, but if he was, he felt no need to tell us. It made no difference as to how we carried out our missions. I commanded a full squad of ten men with Jeremiah and his M60, and was commissioned to follow orders, regardless of what was happening elsewhere in the country.

In order to give the uninitiated a more complete picture of Jeremiah's abilities with the M60, I probably should describe the workings of that weapon. Some battles only make sense with the right picture in mind of what a weapon can do. The Army used the M1 through numerous wars until the M14, 7.62 mm (.308 in) replaced it as the standard-issue rifle in 1959. The M14, 44 inches long, weighed ten pounds fully loaded. The M16, 39 inches long and weighing 8 pounds, 13 ounces, fully loaded with thirty rounds, replaced it in 1964. The Army and Marines began using the M14, the "battle rifle," at the start of the Vietnam war and slowly switched to the M16, the "assault rifle." The M16 round, lighter than the other rounds, explodes into numerous pieces inside the body when it hits a human target. I trained with both the M14 and M16, but used the M16 in combat.

The M60 was a gas-operated, air-cooled, belt-fed killing machine. Nobody wanted to carry "the pig." Weighing 23 pounds with the attached bipod, it was a monster to carry. And the gunner ranked as the enemy's number one target. With its maximum range of 1200 yards, it spit death out with 550 rounds a minute, each with a muzzle velocity of 2,750 feet per second. A tracer round followed every four normal rounds, unless the gunner had loaded the magazine with armor-piercing rounds.

Then add the minimum 100 rounds of belt-fed ammo, which weighed six pounds. The 7.62 mm round serviced both the M14 and the M60. One belt of ammo contained 100 rounds, and an ammo box held 15 separate belts. At 500 rounds a minute, a gunner could empty an ammo box in three minutes with the assistant gunner snapping two belts together every twelve seconds before the gunner had emptied the magazine of each 100-round belt.

Jeremiah's arms were so big, that he could pick up the M60 with one hand, fire it, and usually hit what he was aiming at. As Jeremiah fired the M60 and sent a round through the barrel and down range, a split second later the magazine spit out the empty cartridge, making room for the next round to follow. One hundred rounds in twelve seconds. I can visualize Johnson, with only those twelve seconds, struggling to snap the next belt of 100 rounds onto the belt of rounds racing through the M60, so Jeremiah could continue his uninterrupted fire.

They choppered us to our position that day. With no place to land, the chopper hovered just a few inches above the ground and we jumped out, weapons and all. Some guys fell down on top of their weapons and gear. Ouch! Some heard their knees crackle. Some landed on the dike that separated two rice paddies. Some landed in the rice paddies. They quickly checked their weapons to see that they still functioned when they pulled them out of the water.

I jumped a bit too soon. Maybe three to four feet up. Water hurts at that height. It wasn't like diving off a diving board. I hit the water hard. I didn't use my weapon to protect me from my fall. I was trying to protect my weapon from the water. The shock knocked me out of breath, but I kept trying to count my men and see if any had hurt themselves. We all made it to the top of the dike and headed toward a clump of trees surrounded by rice paddies.

The lieutenant and Wayne had gone on ahead to set up the perimeter.

A few minutes later, Jeremiah began screaming, "I'm gonna die! I'm gonna die!"

I got to him, but he looked very much alive. I had to order him to stop yelling and tell me what was wrong. As he was checking his gear from his jump out of the chopper, he noticed that one of his M26 grenade pins had been pulled free and was lost. His web belt held the grenade in place against his body and the grenade lever closed. Jeremiah was sweating bullets and his muscles were quivering and shaking like jelly.

He had yelled so loudly, that I could see the lieutenant looking back in our direction. I calmed Jeremiah down, and sent word to the lieutenant that everything was under control.

I turned and spoke to the others to back up. We are going to have a live grenade here. They all backed up and crouched down. I carefully inched my fingers under his web belt and took a firm grip on the grenade and the lever together. Then with my other hand I slipped my combat knife under the web belt and sliced it apart. I don't remember if Jeremiah was holding it, or if it fell to the ground, but I was now holding a grenade that had no pin.

When a grenade lever is released, it pops up, strikes and ignites a percussion cap that creates a small spark. That spark ignites the chemicals in the grenade that explode within a couple seconds. I don't know if any one ever tried to release the lever so slowly that it didn't strike and ignite the percussion cap. Jeremiah was shaking and in tears, and I was in no mood to test my ability to disarm a live grenade.

I pushed Jeremiah down onto the ground, turned and threw it as far into the rice paddy as I could, while yelling, "Grenade!" Then I fell down next to Jeremiah while pulling my helmet down over my right ear. The grenade exploded.

As we got to our feet, I said, "Jeremiah, that can happen to anybody in a jungle war. Branches reach out and grab you."

Jeremiah worshipped me from that point on, until I finally had to tell him to stop thanking me. The lieutenant only chuckled when I told him what had happened.

The lieutenant placed me and three guys in a foxhole on the edge of the clump of trees very much in the open, but Jeremiah and his M60 were placed on a small ridge behind us, in a foxhole surrounded by trees. He had a clear view of the rice paddy and the adjoining jungle in front of us. A frontal assault was rare. We depended on spotter planes to tell us the enemy's position.

FEBRUARY 5, 1968, My 20th birthday.

I woke up at 7 a.m. It wasn't raining, but it was hot and humid. My three guys were still sleeping in the foxhole. One was a young Afro-American kid who had managed to lie about his age when he enlisted. He had been in the Army for almost a year, and he was barely seventeen. I couldn't imagine why the Army would take someone underage, but later it became clear that the Army was desperate for ground-pounders by this time in the war. I don't remember those guys' names.

I climbed out of the foxhole toward the ridge, checking to see that Jeremiah was still on the ridge. He sat behind his M60, apparently dozing. I started rummaging through my gear to find the C-Rations.

All of a sudden, a voice echoed in my head, "Put your helmet on."

I looked around to see who was speaking to me. Nobody within shouting range. I continued to rummage.

The voice spoke a second time, louder. "Put your helmet on.

Was I losing it? Maybe I was just hungry, or still tired, or under tension without realizing it. I looked around. Nobody. I kept rummaging.

The voice came close to exploding the third time. "Put. Your. Helmet. On!"

I didn't need to look around. No one was playing any tricks on me. The lieutenant was too far away to be giving me orders. No other E-5 sergeant, who had the authority to yell at me, was close enough to do so. There was no enemy activity. Safe and sound. I was losing it.

Our helmets were heavy. In hot and humid weather, they raised the temperature on our heads. We had no serious complaints about our helmets, but why wear a helmet when nobody is shooting at you? I put my helmet on.

Suddenly, I found myself lying on the ground. I don't even remember the explosion. The first thing I heard was screaming. My three men. The young Afro-American guy was crying out that he wanted his Mamma.

I rolled over, stayed down, and yelled up at Jeremiah on the ridge, "Jeremiah! Shoot anything in the jungle that moves!"

He opened fire, devastating every caterpillar on every

limb on every tree on the rim of the jungle.

I yelled at the kid to stop screaming for his mother, or I would shoot him myself. I think I told him that he was giving away our position, which was ridiculous, since our foxhole was out in the open.

More guys opened fire into the tree line. Somebody fired some tracers into an area of the jungle, and Jeremiah obliterated that area. I loved having him on our side.

My three guys had stopped screaming and were moaning. I slung my M16 over my back, left my gear, crawled over to the foxhole, grabbed one of the guys and started pulling him out of the foxhole. I started yelling, "Tell the medic I'm bringing him some work!"

We didn't like calling for the medics to come to us. They got shot a lot, and there were too few of them. We loved our medics. Gutsy and courageous. We always tried to bring our wounded to them. I had met one medic who told me that he was a CO, Conscientious Objector. A CO wouldn't use a weapon. He didn't believe in killing another person, but he would heal people as a medic. This medic said that he didn't have it inside himself to kill another person. He believed that man was basically good, and that we needed to educate ourselves out of our evil. And the guy clearly was a good person, by anybody's standards. He and I argued a lot about the nature of humanity, but we never convinced each other to change our opinions. One night the Vietcong attacked, and one of his friends was killed, right before his eyes. In the middle of the fight, in a rage, he jumped into a foxhole with a Vietcong and killed him with his bare hands. When the battle was over, no words passed between us. We just looked at each other in sorrow. His commander transferred him to another unit the next day. I've always wondered what plagued him more about that incident: the death of his friend, or the realization of what a good human being is capable of.

After I carried my first guy up the hill, I left him with the medic and went back down for the next guy. The bullets were zipping past our heads from the jungle at about four feet above the ground. Standing up meant that one became holey very quickly. Jeremiah was still doing his thing.

I reached the foxhole, pulled the kid out, and dragged him up the hill. He had stopped screaming and had begun whimpering. In the middle of a firefight, I felt sorry for him. He should have never left home. But then maybe he had come from a crime-infested ghetto where a gang member might have killed him anyway. I never asked. The medic took him off my hands, and I went back down the hill for the third guy.

I think the third guy was conscious, and I didn't have to drag him up the hill. We both crouched and made it to a foxhole just behind Jeremiah. I don't remember being physically exhausted helping the guy up the hill.

Jeremiah had ceased firing. Our forces were firing mortar rounds into the jungle. I turned the third guy over to the medic. I rolled into a foxhole on the ridge.

I passed out. One of my guys behind me jarred me awake by asking me, "Sarge, are you dead?"

I really didn't know how to answer that question. I think I mumbled, "No, I'm not dead."

Then I felt very wet on my left side. It hadn't been raining, and I hadn't slept in a rice patty. I unbuttoned my shirt, stuck my right hand inside, and pulled my hand out. It was covered in bright red liquid.

The thought went through my head. "This is my blood, on the outside of my body. This is not a good thing."

The firefight was over. I got up and walked over to Wayne and Lieutenant Pershing. They looked at my right hand.

"Did you get wounded?" one of them asked.

"Looks like it," I mumbled, looking at my hand. I added something like, "but there's no pain, so it can't be that bad." The medic came over and pulled my shirt open and off my left shoulder. There were numerous pinpoints of blood forming on very small holes on the backside of my left shoulder. I moved my shoulder in a small circle. It didn't hurt. I think I said that I'll be fine.

Pershing told me to get on the Medevac chopper that was taking the wounded back to the field hospital. I told him that I wouldn't do that. He needed me here. My men needed me here. There weren't enough squad leaders with any kind of experience to go around. I was staying.

He gave me a direct order. I told him that most officers got killed because they didn't listen to their squad leaders. He was good man, and I wanted to stay around to try and keep him alive.

Pershing wasn't the typical arrogant young second lieutenant. Pershing wasn't insecure, but he knew his limits. He listened to his men before ordering them forward. Wayne seemed the closest to him. He openly discussed everything with Wayne, even philosophy. I could have been jealous, but I knew nothing of philosophy at that point and didn't want to make a fool of myself displaying my ignorance. Pershing had advised both of us, that if we were going to stay in the Army, we needed to go to Officer Candidate School. In my personal experience, Pershing was a very unusual officer. I didn't want him to die.

Wayne stepped in. "Schneider, get on the chopper."

I went back down the hill to the foxhole, picked up my gear, went back up to Wayne and Pershing, saluted and climbed on the chopper. I don't remember saying goodbye to anyone.

6. FEBRUARY 5 - MARCH 20-ish: REPRIEVE

When the chopper set us down, I jumped off the chopper and helped carry one of my guys on a stretcher. Remember the guy to whom I had given the clerk job? We ran into each other. Small world. Before proceeding to the field hospital, I asked him if my E-5 orders had come in yet. He said, no, but he promised to have those orders sent to me as soon as they came in. He had been keeping an eye on the mail and expected them any day now. He would do everything he could to make sure that I received them, no matter where I ended up outside the country of Vietnam. The rank of E-5 had a lot more privileges than E-4. If I ended up having any free time, E-5 would give me more clout on and off the base.

I arrived at the base hospital. By now my shoulder was letting me know that it wasn't happy. A medic filled out the forms and had me undress. I had bled more than I realized. Messy. I still had my helmet on. I had forgotten to take it off. Funny. The helmet came in two parts. The steel outer shell, and the softer cardboard fiber inner shell. The inner shell had webbing that could be adjusted to fit each head more comfortably, comfort being a relative term with combat gear.

I took it off and removed the inner shell. A small, but discernible, "clink" sounded inside the hard, outer shell. I looked down and saw a small piece of metal shrapnel, that was slightly bigger than a pin head. Still holding the outer steel shell, I put the inner shell down and picked up the piece of shrapnel. I turned the outer steel shell over and saw a small hole in the left side of the helmet. A thin stream of light passed through the hole. I put the piece of shrapnel up to the hole and realized that it had made that hole. I put the outer shell back on my head, placed my finger on the hole, then removed the outer shell and let my finger touch my head at the point of that hole. The piece of shrapnel would have penetrated my head right at the temple, just above eye level. Still holding the piece of shrapnel, I put the outer shell down and examined the inner shell. There was a very small dent on the outside of the cardboard fiber. The outer shell had absorbed the main force of the shrapnel, and the inner shell had stopped the piece from sending me into the next world. I should have kept that piece of shrapnel.

People have often asked me where that voice came from. I usually encourage them to think about the spiritual realm as the main possibility. If God does exist, as I believe He does, isn't it logical that He can use words to communicate with us when He wants to? I'm just glad that He didn't give up trying to get my attention, and that I listened to Him the third time.

The surgeon put me under and removed eleven pieces of shrapnel from my left shoulder. He left one piece inside because it had lodged itself so deeply into my shoulder that it almost touched a lung. He said that the body was built to protect itself, and because the piece was small, the body would wrap it up to keep it from moving toward any vital parts. I still wanted to study physics if I lived through Vietnam, and I wondered if I would attract magnets.

Years later, a doctor took an X-ray of my chest because of a bad cold. He came out and gently, but directly, informed me that he was sorry to have to tell me that I had tuberculosis. I smiled and told him that if he used a magnifying glass to take a closer look at that black spot, the words "Made in China" would jump off his X-ray negative. He laughed in relief and replied, "Ah, shrapnel!"

In 2018, another X-ray showed that there are two pieces wrapped up near my lung. Don't know if they missed a piece, or if the one piece split off into two. At 71, I'm not worried about it. Other more vital things are beginning to fall apart.

The surgeon in Vietnam bandaged me up, gave me some pain pills and said I would probably heal in four to six weeks. Then he sent me to processing. The Tet Offensive, which I still didn't know about, had filled all the hospitals in Vietnam, and, therefore, they were sending me to the

Philippines.

I arrived at Clark Airbase, and they promptly placed me in a ward with a bunch of other wounded GIs. Generic field beds, but the nurses smiled, and the food was gourmet compared to the C-Rations. The pills did their job, the pain died down, and I got bored. The number of casualties overwhelmed the kind and helpful nurses, so they had no time to engage our minds.

I woke up the second day to discover that the spaces between the beds had shrunk. More casualties. A nurse squeezed her white bottom between our beds to give me some medicine. I made eye contact with the guy who had just been brought it. We both smiled at the nurse's gyrations as she maneuvered in the narrow aisle between our beds. When she left, I noted that he looked in worse shape than me. I asked, "You're still alive?"

Pain surfaced on his face as he struggled to shift position on the bed. "Yes. Death came calling, but I wasn't home."

We joked and chatted with each other while watching the nurses squeeze between beds to take care of more and more patients.

A nurse brought us both a copy of the local military newspaper. Normally, the information was vague and indefinite, but if something happened to someone important, it made the news. My unit made the news. Who was important in my unit?

Lieutenant Pershing. One of our men had gone missing, and Lieutenant Pershing had gone out alone to find him. He was killed in the process.

I wavered from being sick and extremely angry. There was nothing in the story about Wayne, so I assumed he was okay, but I wanted to destroy something. Pershing was a good man. He should never have had to fight in that war. What an incredible waste of a man's life. What about all the good things he could have done if he had lived? What about having kids and raising them in a world of peace? What about living long enough to help your parents enter the grave, and have your own children say goodbye to you after a long, satisfying life of hard work, ending in contentment?

Pershing and I weren't even friends, yet I seethed. I didn't cry. It wouldn't do any good anyway. Just move on. Maybe someday I'll start getting depressed when bad things happen, but so far, internal anger has been my fallback. Just move on. Remember, Floyd, to whom you belong. Let Him handle it. I hate this world, and yet my own evil heart is part of the problem. Move on.

The only clothes I possessed were my undershorts and white nightgown. I had broken one of the ear pieces on my glasses. They barely hung on my ears. I had my wallet with just over $18 left over from my last paycheck on February 1st. I have no idea where I spent less than $2 in Vietnam, or how I could have even gotten change.

I was well enough to go to the bathroom without any supervision. I waited until all the head nurses were gone and the other nurses were too busy to notice. Dressed in just my white nightgown, I put on those cheap, disposable, white hospital slippers, grabbed my wallet, and walked off the base into town. Very low security back then. The war was in Vietnam, not the Philippines.

The pain pills were doing their job, and my legs worked fine, so I walked a couple miles until I bumped into a small shopping mall. Cool. I went straight to an eye glass shop. The man behind the counter looked like he was in charge. I asked him what it would cost to have my glasses fixed. Everybody stopped and stared. He took the glasses, disappeared into the back room, fixed them, returned, gave them back to me, and asked me if I had just arrived from combat in Vietnam. I don't suppose he had any other customers showing up in a hospital gown. I said yes. With a slight salute, he replied, "On the house." Other people in the shop mumbled some affirmative noises. I thanked him, closed my wallet, and left.

I walked into another shop and bought a couple of shirts, dress jeans, socks, shorts and comfortable walking shoes. Everyone stared in awe of a soldier in a white nightgown walking around buying clothes. Most of the shops gave me everything free of charge. With almost $18 still in my wallet, I walked back to the hospital in the nightgown. I could have changed clothes at the mall, but I might have had to produce some identification at the hospital gate, and a nightgown would get me in quicker. I got a mild scolding from the head nurse, but when she looked at the other nurses, who should have shown disapproval, she just giggled. My dinner tray arrived with an extra bowl of ice cream for dessert that evening. I think they were tickled that I had pulled that off.

I was shipped off immediately to Japan. The beds were filling up in the Philippines, and I suppose they figured that if I could walk into town on my own, they needed the bed for someone less fortunate.

From little research I've done in writing this book, I think I ended up at Camp Zama, Japan, the Army military base/hospital. The Navy and the Marines had their own bases elsewhere in Japan.

The day I arrived, I received my E-5 promotion in the mail. That clerk was good to his word. Those orders had chased me all the way through the Philippines. Then I read the promotion letter more closely. I had been awarded a Purple Heart for being wounded in combat. Then I read that Lieutenant Pershing had recommended me for the Army Commendation Medal for courage under fire.

I looked at that letter for a long time. I hadn't done anything spectacular. I had told my gunner to shoot people, and I had carried three guys back to the command post so the medic could take care of them. Stooping down under four feet to avoid bullets wasn't courageous. It was intelligent. I had argued with Pershing about staying in the field because he needed me to help keep him alive. Nothing spectacular. Just doing my job and wishing that I could have hindered him from looking for that dead soldier and getting killed. Anger consumed me.

The Army doctor who treated me in Japan was a captain. I wasn't in a lot of pain, and he wasn't interested in promoting his rank. He gave me a general physical exam before examining my stitches. We started talking about the topic of doubt, and somehow the conversation shifted to God. He didn't believe in God because he couldn't see him. He had me lay down on a cot on my stomach so he could examine my stitches. There was a table of medical tools right in front of me with some needles within reach. He turned away, I reached up, grabbed a needle, turned over just enough to jab him in the bottom. Not really hard, but he yelped, and I said, "You can't believe in pain, because you can't see it."

He didn't explode in anger, just rubbed his backside, and when he checked over my stitches, he pushed and shoved and jerked them a bit more than necessary. I kept protesting, "Ouch, I believe in pain even if I can't see it. Lighten up!" He finally began to chuckle. The next day the grumpy head nurse, a major, asked me what I had done to their doctor. She related that he had finished out the rest of his day yesterday smiling. I enjoy making people laugh, but there are limits.

The nurse showed surprise that he wanted to see me the next day. Neither of us recounted the previous conversation, but he was smiling. He released me and told me to come back in a week for another check-up. As I was leaving, I asked the grumpy major head nurse if there was any possibility that I could leave the base. Her body language spoke louder than her words. The only place I was going from that hospital was back to Vietnam.

Whatever.

I immediately went to the hospital PX, bought three stripes and had them sewn on my shirts. I now proudly wore E-5 stripes as a non-Commissioned officer. I saw the captain the next week. He confirmed the diagnosis of the surgeon, who had pulled out the shrapnel in the field hospital in Nam, that I could go back to killing people in four to five weeks.

I begged him to give me permission to leave the hospital compound and go to the PX on the base. I told him that I wasn't going to apologize for my needle illustration since he clearly got the point, but I mentioned that I was going insane with inactivity. After all, coming off of combat and having absolutely nothing to do was deadly for the psyche. I don't remember if he smiled or not, but he informed the grumpy major that he was giving me permission to leave the hospital compound. She was not happy, but when it came to diagnosis and treatment of a patient, apparently an MD captain outranked a non-MD major. I never saw him again. A different doctor took out my stitches and a nurse processed me out a few weeks later.

Immediately after the major had informed me of the captain's wrong decision to release me upon the world off base, I jumped on the bus and descended on the non-Commissioned officers club. I found the notices board, and I read every non-duty activity being offered to the enlisted men on the base. I think that the base had one large building that housed the PX, a large area for card game tournaments, and a huge stage for performances attached to a restaurant. As it turned out, Army patients were allowed all of these pleasures. They just couldn't leave the base. Other patients had had similar encounters with Grumpy.

I spent just under six weeks there. At some point, I bought some Japanese steak knives and had them shipped back home to Mom with a long letter telling her how good things were. I said little about being wounded. I played tourist for one day and took pictures of big fat stone buddhas. I stumbled into some Pinochle games with some other bored GIs. At the Pinochle tables, I met two other guys who were just trying to make it through their enlistment. The three of us chose to have dinner together at the restaurant. That evening the management had rearranged the tables for a stage band and an open area for dancing. The place filled up quickly. I believe that the Army realized that boredom is one of a soldier's worst enemies. They didn't train us for boredom. The Army did their best to keep their wounded entertained.

I love chocolate. Chocolate doesn't curb my appetite. It's simply a separate category of food that carries me through life by adding an additional pleasure between C-Rations and gourmet meals. Many years later, I lived in Austria, and for fifteen years I contributed heavily to the upkeep of the chocolate industry in Europe.

At the restaurant on the base, I had consumed a couple chocolate candy bars before our meal arrived. The waiter offered us some hard liquor. The other guys took some, but I had seldom even drunk any wine or beer before. I said yes. Since I didn't know what was what, they gave me some bourbon. It tasted a little bitter, but sweet. I liked it. I wouldn't tell Mom. She would worry that it might become a habit. Years earlier, one of her cousins had publicly chided her for refusing to go along with the crowd and drink some wine. She held her ground, and eventually watched that cousin destroy his family by becoming an alcoholic. She never made fun of him. She just didn't want her one and only son starting down that road.

I don't remember accepting a third glass. I don't remember getting back to the hospital barracks. I didn't get arrested or busted. I just woke up the next morning in my bunk, returned to the club, and found one of the guys I had gone to the club with the night before. He told me that it probably had been the combination of chocolate and bourbon. He smiled when I asked him what I had done after the second glass. He just replied that I was very funny, but I hadn't done anything really stupid or ruined their evening. He and a buddy had taken me back to the barracks. I thanked him, but he wouldn't tell me what he meant by "stupid, but not *really* stupid."

I went back to the notice board. It was February. In the coming weeks those in charge of keeping the off-duty soldiers busy were sponsoring a ski trip for Army personnel. It didn't say, "No patients." It just said Army personnel. I signed up and showed up. I considered the ski trip providential as my own birthday present to myself. Skiing replaced Shrapnel.

It seems that Camp Zama and Mt. Kusatu are over six hours drive apart. If that is true, then we would have gotten up very early in the morning to arrive on the slopes with any time left over to have a good day of skiing.

I fell in love. Nancy was the nurse directing the excursion. I managed to sit next to her for some of the time on the bus. I discovered that she also loved Jesus. She loved serving the wounded. It pained her to witness their suffering. Did I say that I fell in love? I kept wondering how we could date after I returned to Vietnam.

She ruled the ski slopes like a queen. I headed toward the "suicide strip" in my attempt to impress her. She made me follow her down that patch of sheer ice to demonstrate how I should navigate the sharp narrow turns that kept challenging the best of skiers who hadn't expected the surprise of solid slippery death under their skis. The difficulty was keeping my focus on the turns instead of her elegant form gracefully navigating the narrow canyons.

We separated and skied together and separated and skied together until I asked her to follow me down the suicide slope to evaluate my improved performance. All went well.

Around four in the afternoon, I had time for just one more run. One last time for the suicide strip. Nancy and I had separated, but she had been adamant about returning our skis and getting to the bus on time or it would leave without us.

I took the leap. About halfway down the slope, one of those canyons appeared with high snow walls and a narrow icy track between them. I had done this twice before. Concentrate. No room for mistakes. No fancy turns. No showing off because no one was watching. Just start slowly at the top because your skis were going to pick up speed toward the bottom, and the point of the exercise was to still be standing when you got to the bottom, which ended at the front door of the lodge.

Since I had made it down twice, still standing, I felt good about myself. If warning bells were going off, I had turned them off. Just as I entered the canyon, I glanced back to see Nancy behind me. One should never look back when death is on the line. I hit the top of the canyon at moderate speed, much faster than recommended. I made it to within sight of the lodge doors. I missed a turn by an inch. Pure ice. I bounced about four times before crumbling into a heap of arms and legs intertwined with skis and ski poles sticking out in all directions right in front of the lodge door at the bottom of the run. Nancy paralleled to a perfect stop right to me.

"You all right?"

Before I could answer, she exclaimed, "You're bleeding!"

I sat up, but it was too cold to feel any liquid on my body.

She moved toward my back, then back to my front and started taking off my rented ski jacket and civilian shirt. A nurse, even on the ski slope. She saw the bandages.

"You're wounded! You're a patient! You're not allowed to leave the base."

There went my dating life. She didn't sit next to me or talk to me on the way back. I spent the whole bus trip back feeling sorry for myself. I shipped back to Vietnam a week later.

7. MARCH 20-ISH – MAY 15, 1968: BACK IN COMBAT

Toward the end of March, 1968, I returned to Bien Hoa. I still knew nothing of the American media's response to the Tet Offensive. Depression had settled into the fabric of everyone around me.

Until my orders came through, all I could do was hang out at the PX/bar on base. One guy played Nancy Sinatra singing "These Boots Are Made For Walking" over and over and over, until I wanted to break the juke box.

The E-5 liaison sergeant's job consisted of serving the GI's living in the cities. A liaison sergeant, who was stationed in Saigon, approached me with an offer to take over his job. In two weeks, he would complete his twelve months, and he was heading home, back to the States.

If I took his job, what would I be doing? His commanding liaison officer travelled a lot and left the sergeant to man the office in Saigon. He spent most of his time running messages between command posts, retrieving and delivering mail to soldiers in the field, and some other odd jobs that an E-3 could do, but there wasn't an E-3 around to do them. Since the Bien Hua Airbase sat on the northeast corner of Saigon, the sergeant seldom left that area. He mentioned that most of the fighting was centered in the north around Hua and Quang Tri. I still didn't know about the Tet Offensive, so I didn't question his comments about any enemy activity around Saigon. He assured me that his job was safe and secure. I could spend the last six and a half months of my tour there in comfort, with little to do but be a messenger boy.

I turned him down. Another insane decision, but I wanted to see who was still alive in my combat unit. I received a message from him later. A week after I left, while he was out delivering a message, a Vietcong mortar round got lucky and evaporated his office.

Back on the field, I was assigned to another Search and Destroy unit. Wayne was still alive and in the same company, but in another platoon. The platoon leader was glad to have an E-5 back as a squad leader. Most of my previous comrades had been wounded or killed. It didn't hurt as much since friendship includes first names, which we seldom chose to learn.

On one of our missions, our company stumbled onto an underground tunnel complex. They told us it was the size of a small town. A slight exaggeration, but when we blew up one of the tunnels, it sent reverberations over 100 yards away. There was no enemy in sight. They had already evacuated the tunnel.

Our soldiers who served as tunnel rats were gutsy. The rest of us referred to them as insane. Long before America arrived, the Vietcong had learned how to entice the French to their death in the underground blackness by cleverly disguising traps intended to maim or kill a soldier who grabbed the wrong stick or stepped on innocent-looking rock.

Whenever we blew tunnels, a soldier would descend into the darkness and set a C-4 charge. Then he would climb out and someone would yell, "Fire in the hole!" Everyone bent down to avoid any flying debris when the C-4 exploded.

As our tunnel rats were blowing the tunnels, I had been directed to take my squad along a tree line next to an open field. Wayne's squad was covering the other tree line.

Wayne was the furthest thing from my mind at that point. I kept my men focused on looking for traps set near any undiscovered tunnels.

Someone yelled, "Fire in the hole!" and I *felt* Wayne take a hit. I *sensed* it. I didn't crouch down, but turned toward his side of the field, saw him and screamed, "Wayne!" Then I saw him buckle at the knees and fall to the ground. There had been no enemy fire. The explosion had sent a piece of metal through the air at bullet speed and hit him in the back of the leg. He was immediately surrounded by his men. I couldn't leave my squad and run across the field to see how he was. They got a medic to him and carried him off to somewhere.

I couldn't even say goodbye. Would he die? Was he wounded enough to keep him from coming back to this hell hole? Conflict raged inside of me. This wasn't supposed to be happening. I had made the mistake of learning his first name. I made the mistake of becoming friends with him, with Wayne. I cared about him. I didn't want him to come back. I cared about me. I wanted him to come back.

Wayne was gone, but life went on. We arrived back at the base. None of my men had been killed. As we congratulated each other for waking up the next morning, we still avoided learning first names.

I don't remember having any expectations when I arrived in Vietnam. I had taken the advice of my high school counselor to spend three years growing up by going into the military, which should prepare me for college. My life-long dream to become a nuclear physicist still permeated my mind whenever I thought about the future.

The closest I had come to the world of death was Mom. And, yet, I wasn't horribly upset about the possibility of Mom dying, just as long as she died with our relationship restored. I hadn't thought about my own death. Here, in Vietnam, death had crept into my world as something that I needed to figure out how to deal with.

Not my own death. If I died, I had progressed enough in my faith in Jesus as my eternal future, that I wasn't worried about that.

I've often wondered why people respond differently when they experience pain and suffering. Some people run to God and others curse Him. I don't believe that God preordains people to make the choices that they make. He will use those choices to bring about His ultimate goals, but how He does that is beyond me. I've just never understood why people reject God's help in desperate times instead of seeking His comfort and support to get through those times.

I've never looked down on my comrades who refused God's assurance or hope of the future. I knew that I was no better than any of them. I just wondered why they didn't see that their bravado, drinking binges, and LSD (a drug that permanently damaged your brain) were nothing more than temporary escapes that only lasted until the next firefight. We all faced the same possibilities of permanent damage or death. A person's future goals in this life, like college or career or marriage offered none of us assurance of coming out of Nam alive.

Therefore, the most important word in everybody's vocabulary was "Short!" The longer you spent in Nam, the less time you had to spend there. "Short" was our code word for waking up and realizing that we had one less day to spend in Vietnam. "Short!" was the word everyone worshipped. Just stay alive long enough to leave. I used that word a lot, too, but most guys didn't want to talk about asking Jesus for help to get them through it all.

I've read a number of books about the experiences of others in Vietnam since I started writing this book. One author described his response to a number of close calls with: "Thank God, that missed me." But when he was wounded in an ambush, he had the thought that if he was going to die, maybe he should acknowledge the existence of God, but he immediately rejected that idea, having previously concluded that there was no such thing. So he just figured he was going to discover what death was like.

I never looked down on these guys. Some of them were brave and humble; others died because they were arrogant and stupid. They didn't listen to their own men. They just didn't have any sense of direction. They needed what I had, but seldom does one listen to a contemporary. Some poured their hearts out to me about their fears and hopeless lives, and I listened as best as an older teenager could, but they seldom accepted my solution. They viewed me as eccentric, and they couldn't relate to my world. They didn't reject me as a person or a soldier. I had learned how to earn their trust along the way by doing the best job I could do, while trying to help others who were struggling.

As I saw more combat and more desperation and more death that didn't have a pattern in who it chose to tap on the shoulder, I became bolder in bringing up the subject of Jesus. My method of introducing the conversations can't be used in an everyday context. I would read my New Testament when another guy could see me.

"Hey, Schneider, what are you reading?"

"The Bible."

"What the f*** are you reading that for?"

"Joe, we're probably all going to die in the next mortar attack. You might think about what you're going to say to God when you meet Him."

"Man, you're weird. There ain't no God."

"That will come as a surprise to Him. Just because you're ignorant about His existence doesn't make Him disappear." Then before he could bury me in another barrage of cuss words, I would add, "Seriously, Joe, why don't you just read a couple of pages." I reached out to hand him my New Testament. "Here, take this one. I can get another one."

Most still laughed, but a few listened. I quickly realized that their response was not my problem. I argued with some. I didn't realize it at the time, but I was using apologetics to win them over. I soon gave up believing that how I approached the subject of Jesus made any difference in their openness and their responses. Some listened because no one else had talked to them about the spiritual world. Others listened because they were being polite to someone they respected in some way. A couple guys hated me. One man threatened to kill me, until I helped him out of a problem. He requested, and received, an immediate transfer to another unit.

Toward the end of my time in Nam, although I did not know it would come to an end so soon, I went to a Catholic priest and asked him if he could supply me with a bunch of Gideon New Testaments. He looked at me as if combat had made me snap, but he found some and gave them to me. I began passing them out to different men in my unit. Some took them just to take them. Some took them with a question mark on their faces but asked nothing. Some asked why. I said, "Because by tomorrow we're probably all going to be dead, and this is the only book that tells you about the next life. Read it carefully."

A couple guys tossed it on the ground. I watched a few start to read Matthew. Our unit moved so much, that there was never enough time for someone to ask me questions about what they were reading. I figured that it was God's responsibility to help them understand what they were reading.

I never grew close to anyone. As men, we joked about a lot of personal stuff, but we never got close. Ever. Those who grew close, died internally when their friend was killed. Distance provided us with our emotional flack jacket. When the message came down, "So-and-so got killed yesterday," we were able to write it off as, "Short!" As a squad leader, I never wanted to know the first names of my men. Just the name on the label on their shirts. Their last names. And when they were no longer in my unit, I forgot those names. I can still remember some of them dying, but I don't remember their names. Names are important. Too much suffering came from knowing their names and remembering the person attached to that name. We had to let their relatives endure all the suffering. When someone died, we shut down the emotions and moved on to the next mission with the guys still alive, the guys we never wanted to care about, and they wouldn't care about me. I didn't have to wonder about what the guys would have said about me if I had died. They would have said nothing.

But God did not create us to be loners. We needed at least one close friend, whose name we knew. For me that was Wayne. Not Moore (his last name).

We began going further north in Vietnam. When my unit arrived at LZ Sally—Landing Zone Sally—peace ruled. Spring was in the air, and when I raised my head to view the jungle all round us, the blossoming colors assaulted my senses. It was beautiful.

A landing zone was just a landing zone. Barren earth littered with crates and equipment and soldiers. No villages. Apparently, the Army had had to clear away the forest to make way for a chopper landing pad. Huge Ch-47 Chinook transport helicopters, which could carry up to 55 soldiers and three M60s, and flew a combat radius of 230 miles, landed, and took off many times a day. We wondered if we were preparing to invade North Vietnam. Everybody wanted to. Most felt that we could have won that war in two weeks if we could have just nuked Hanoi. The upper echelon paid no attention to us.

I got over the beauty of the jungle once patrols began again. LZ Sally became our home away from home when we returned from those patrols. Before I had been wounded on Feb. 5th, in late January, my unit had driven through the small town of Quang Tri in the north. I think that our company was being used as support for the main American forces in the area. I remember how beautiful the few buildings had been. I discovered later that although it was a market town, it was also the capital of Quang Tri province and very important to the South Vietnamese people.

My company wasn't part of the battle, but the Vietcong initiated a crucial attack against Quang Tri on January 31, the day of the Tet Offensive. Our troops devastated the Vietcong within twenty-four hours. After I returned from Japan, my unit drove through Quant Tri again. We didn't engage the enemy at that point because there wasn't much left to fight for. All the buildings had been destroyed. I was told that a beautiful library had been evaporated by the Vietcong during the battle. I sometimes wondered what mankind could accomplish if he would stop going to war.

The biggest battle during the Tet Offensive was in the city of Hue, the cultural and spiritual capital of the country. Whoever owned Hue, owned Vietnam. Hue was so significant to the Vietcong, that they dared to break that seven-day cease fire in hopes of taking over the city that held the most spiritual significance in their nation. Six thousand Vietcong attacked the city that held just a handful of Marines and one elite Vietnamese unit. The Vietcong knew how to fight an urban war, one building at a time.

Our units had not been trained in that type of combat. The Detroit riots had brought us close to viewing what urban combat was like, but nothing had prepared our guys for this battle. Undermanned and outgunned, the Marines took a lot of casualties. Eventually, reinforcements showed up, and those Marines who had been raised in the city and understood street fighting, took command and led the way. Sometimes a private would lead a squad sergeant and his lieutenant around the corner to take the next alley, street, or building. It took our guys almost four weeks to retake the city, one building at a time. We lost 218, with almost 1,400 wounded. The enemy lost between 1,000 and 5,000 dead, depending on which news report one listened to. Most of us believed, that the phrase, "winning a battle, but losing a war," came from the American News Media who, in their attempt to become America's moral compass, exchanged simply reporting the news for arguing that this battle proved that America was losing the war. Historians are still arguing over that issue.

The saddest part of that battle was the civilian devastation. Most of the innocent Vietnamese were killed by the North Vietcong. Some were killed as the Vietcong used them as shields against American fire.

My unit was not called in to help with that battle. When I returned to the battlefield in late March, that one was over. Again, I have no natural answer to the question as to why I was removed from Vietnam during that time. I know that, although I wanted to go home, I would have wanted to be a part of those reinforcements who saved our men from the Vietcong.

After returning to LZ Sally from a patrol, the Vietcong took their turn and sent us some mortar rounds. We lost some crates, and our medics had their hands full. As our spotter planes located the enemy positions, our mortars answered theirs, and our gunships arrived and decimated the enemy. With the battle over, the medics were grateful for our help in taking care of the wounded.

My step-brother, Jim, had enlisted a few weeks after me. I told him that he was more intelligent to go through basic training when the weather was better. He ended up in an engineer battalion, and, if I remember correctly, we ran into each other at LZ Sally. We were both glad that we were still alive. He told me that he was smarter than me because I was always being assigned to Search and Destroy missions. He got to hide behind some armor whenever the fireworks started. I think he lasted the entire twelve months. He's still alive and well today. Just a few years later, I was given the privilege of helping him and his wife, Judy, to join the kingdom of Jesus.

At LZ Sally, I determined to start giving out New Testaments to any of the guys who would listen to me. I found another Catholic priest who agreed to supply me with some more New Testaments. I should have been impressed that he was that far north, but I didn't ask if he had volunteered for that location or if he was just unlucky. He gave me the same puzzled look as the previous chaplain, but he came through with the New Testaments. When I picked them up, I asked him if he had read the New Testament. I don't remember his answer.

While I was stationed at LZ Sally, we were hearing rumors that the South Korean troops really wanted to win this war, and they chose not to abide by the Rules of the Geneva Convention.[1] I knew nothing about who those troops answered to for their combat activities.

The rumors appealed to most of us because of the rumored results of the South Korean combat tactics in the

---

[1] In 1929, ten years after the end of World War I, some scholars wrote up some humanitarian rules about how people should or should not kill each other. More scholars updated those rules in 1949 after the end of World War II. Enforcing that law is obviously problematic. Most cultures see the purpose of war as killing the enemy and winning the war, using any available means possible.

field. The South Koreans would play on the animistic religious views of the Vietcong by cutting off some body parts of dead Vietcong soldiers and displaying them in the open for all to see.

Why did this affect the Vietcong? They believe that when a person dies, they don't cease to exist, but pass into another world. Their physical bodies play a role in what happens to them in the next world. The variety of their beliefs is almost innumerable but losing a body part and not receiving a proper burial seemed to keep a person from enjoying the next life in some way.[2]

If the rumors were true, the South Koreans apparently understood how to use the Vietcong religion against them in combat. This led to the rumor that when the Vietcong realized that they were facing a South Korean unit in combat, the Vietcong would flee the field as quickly as possible.

None of this information affected me personally. At that time, I didn't know or really care how the war would turn out. I wanted to go home, but as long as I had to stay there, I chose to make the best of it.

After I picked up about a dozen New Testaments to add to my gear, I started handing them out to my own squad in hopes that they would read a few pages before throwing them away. I don't think I had any left when I was finally wounded for the last time and shipped out.

Wayne showed up. He hadn't died, and his wound had healed quickly. When he came back, he was assigned to the same company but a different platoon. I still remembered his name, but I figured that if he got killed in the next firefight, it wouldn't hurt as much.

By this time, we were both old-timers. Our unit was short on old-timers. I didn't know it at the time, but I only had a few weeks left in Nam.

---

[2] Various websites explain the complexity of this kind of animistic religion. https://asiasociety.org/education/religion-vietnam.

8. May 15, 1968: Last Day

Someone finally told us about the organized Tet Offensive, and that the Vietcong had taken a severe blow during those four weeks. In hindsight, that was true, but that didn't mean that the remaining enemy troops were going to lay down their guns and go home.

However, word came down that our unit was scheduled for a week of R & R, Rest and Recuperation. How much money a person had determined how far away from the war zone one could travel, there and back. We packed and the trucks arrived to transport us to Saigon the next day. Our orders told us to make the most of a week's vacation, then return and regroup in Bien Hoa for our next combat assignment.

I dreamed of SCUBA diving off the coast of Australia. One day of flying to Sydney or Brisbane, five days of diving on the Great Barrier Reef off the northeast coast of Australia, and one day of flying back into a world where one lived from minute to minute. I had given no thought to the feasibility of my plan. I just wanted out at least for a few days.

Before the trucks started their engines on the morning of the next day, a major announced that our departure would delayed by half a day. Reports had come in of possible activity in a village not far from our unit, and he wanted to just check it out. I remember him emphasizing that if we did run into the enemy, the only thing that mattered was body count, i.e., how many could we kill. That attitude made sense considering how many men we had lost during the Tet Offensive. The major assured us that we would experience little contact with a combat force, and that we would be out of there by noon.

We and the Vietcong spent the next two days killing each other.

Before loading into the choppers, we had received some new recruits. I don't know if they had been slated to go on R & R with the rest of us. Our company normally had 200 men in four platoons of fifty each. My squad had ten guys plus the gunnery team. Some in each squad carried M79 grenade launchers as their primary weapons. That weapon could noiselessly send a grenade a long way into the enemy position. All you heard was the round going off, then nothing, then the explosion. You could never tell from where the round was coming.

The new recruits had enlarged my squad by four men. All four men had arrived in Vietnam the day before. They had come straight out of Advanced Infantry Training. They were all E-3s. I felt old.

We got into the choppers and flew to some rice paddies outside of a village. A large stream, almost a small river, ran along one side of the village. Three tree lines formed a huge square around the rice paddy on our side of the village. Trees and jungle hindered our view of the village.

Apart from the sounds of our own noise, serenity ruled. There was no enemy in sight. We could get back in the choppers, and I could fly to Australia, probably on a military transport.

Most of the company fanned out along the tree line that paralleled the village. I was directed to place my squad on the edge of that outer tree line and the left tree line. My squad would be the point squad for entering the village from that direction. But if there was no enemy to be seen, why weren't we getting back into the choppers?

A ditch ran parallel along and outside that left tree line. The ditch had to have been man-made. It was well-formed. It was deep enough for a man to stand up in it and just see over the edge in both directions. It was wide enough for six men to stand side-by-side in it. I noticed a mound of dirt at the other end of the ditch. It reached the top of the ditch. It looked like a dam. I couldn't see over it.

Hurry up and wait. We're just going to be here for an hour or two. I began talking to one of the new guys. He started to tell me all about himself, but I cut him off by asking him what he thought about God. I still didn't want the pain of knowing too much about him if he got killed, but no one objected to my efforts to engage people on the subject of Jesus. I wasn't the only follower of Jesus in my unit, but the other ones were more low-key than myself.

By this time, I didn't care what anybody thought about me or my faith. If I was right, and they objected, they needed to discuss the evidence with me. Usually no one objected. They just didn't want to talk about it, so we changed the subject. Friendship Evangelism had no place in a war zone. I didn't need to become their friend to share the eternal good news with them. It was the good news they really needed, not my emotional support, especially since I was probably going to die and leave them with what? My friendship? And what would they remember? A nice guy, just like them? Lost and wondering what life was all about? Some people label any follower of Jesus as aggressive who verbally shares the Good News with another person. They seem to view any verbal communication about the Good News with strangers as aggressive. It just didn't make any sense to not talk about Jesus, since most of us were facing certain death any time now anyway.

This new guy and I discussed Jesus for about twenty minutes. I gave him a New Testament. I told him to give serious thought to what I'd said and to start reading it as soon as we got out of this rice paddy. He nodded. My E-6 called me over to his position.

"Schneider, we're doing this in two waves. One squad is following the other tree line," he pointed across the square rice paddy, "and you're going to take your squad along this one." He pointed toward that mound of dirt. I didn't feel brave. I wasn't afraid. I wasn't mentally processing what I was doing internally. I was just automatically turning off the emotions and getting the job done. Like flipping a switch and moving forward. If there was any exhilaration, it was based on simply wondering what was going to happen next.

I returned to my squad. "Saddle up. We're scouting

along this ditch toward the village. Lock and load. Safeties off. Eyes open for any movement to our left front, straight ahead of us and across that corner of the rice patty into the village," which we couldn't see very well due to the trees on our right and the trees in front of the village. I positioned the men behind me in the order I believed where they would do the most good. It's hard to conceal fourteen men well. I told Jeremiah to stay on the corner to cover us if we started taking fire from our corner of the village. I wasn't worried about the other corner. The other squad had to deal with that. Randal usually carried the second M60, but for some reason he was near my squad and carrying an M79 that day. Maybe an officer gave the M60 to someone else who weighed more than 150 pounds.

I placed the guy I had just spoken with right behind me. I made sure that his weapon was ready and that his finger was not on the trigger, so he wouldn't shoot me in the back by accident. I remember our one-sided conversation. I coached him. "So do exactly as I do. If I step here, you step here. If I turn here, you turn here. If I squat and take a crap, you squat and take a crap. If I do something that gets me dead, you don't do that. Clear?"

He just nodded and looked at the ground.

I turned and started walking along the left side of the ditch. As I mentioned earlier, the ditch was ten feet across and at least four feet deep, and it stretched straight along the tree line until it reached that mound, which I could not see over.

I kept thinking, hang onto the high ground. You can't see anything if you're in the ditch. The new guy was three feet behind me.

I kept looking at that mound of dirt at the end of the ditch. A small tree about four inches wide stood on the very edge of the ditch, and it obstructed my vision of the mound slightly. With my right hand, I continued to point my M16 toward the mound. I reached out with my left hand across the M16 and grabbed the tree. I wanted to stay out of the ditch. I wanted to stay on the high ground. I was going to pull my body to the left around the tree, while keeping my eyes and my weapon focused on the mound. I wasn't looking to my left, since other units had that direction covered.

None of my training had prepared me for what happened next. There was too much silence. I hadn't registered that all the animal noises had disappeared. I kept looking at that mound. My trigger finger had grown accustomed to lightly resting itself on that piece of curved metal that would automatically anticipate the brain impulse to push it backwards and send those lethal bullets down range. My whole body tensed, waiting for that split second when the world would change.

Before I could pull myself around the tree and place it behind me, *something* pushed me on the left arm and literally shoved me downwards into the ditch. I didn't have time to look left. I stumbled and for a second, I looked at the ground because I was fighting to keep my balance. I managed to stand up part way and look up at the mound.

I saw a ball of yellow and red flames slowly rotating directly at me. One or two seconds? No time to be afraid. Just enough time to register what I was seeing. A rocket was coming straight at me. The only thing that entered my mind was, "Oops."

I found myself sitting on the ground in the ditch. I looked up at the mound. I looked at my chest and stomach. I was still holding the M16. My trigger finger was squeezing the life out of the trigger. With my left hand, I felt my body. No holes. No blood. "Is this what's it's like to be dead?" I asked myself. I wasn't dead.

I looked at my weapon and released the trigger. For some reason I had put a magazine of tracer bullets in my M16. Tracer bullets left a red trail in the air, and we used these tracer bullets to show the M60 gunner where to shoot. I don't remember why I had put that magazine in my M16, but I remember seeing all those red lines go down range and hit something sticking up just above the mound of dirt. I had emptied the entire magazine at the person who had fired the rocket.

MOVE! As I jumped up, I put another magazine in my M16. Standing in the ditch, I kept looking at the mound. I became aware of jabbing pain in the back of my legs. I stepped back and to my left. I began screaming for Randal to get behind me and cover me with his grenade launcher. With my eyes still on the mound and my weapon ready and pointed in the right direction, I attempted to step up out of the ditch to my left. To steady myself, I put my left hand down on the ground on the top side of the ditch.

My hand didn't hit dirt. It hit something soft and squishy. It took a second to process the sight of a dead body without a head.

The soldier behind me had not followed my orders. Instead of grabbing the tree, keeping it between him and the mound, and thus following me into the ditch, he had grabbed the tree with his left hand and started to pull himself around the tree. He hadn't been keeping his eyes on me or the mound. The rocket hit him squarely on his left shoulder.

Cuss words filled the air. I yelled for two other guys to come get the dead soldier. The pain in the back of my legs was becoming acute. Randal showed up. I instructed him to put some grenade rounds in the trees directly above the mound, so anybody who tried to ambush us again would be decimated by a grenade.

He got in a hurry. Overenthusiastic. The M79 worked like this. Point the weapon up into the trees just above our heads, open the breach by keeping the stock pointing toward the top of the trees and lowering the barrel. This move pointed the barrel toward the trees above the mound. Insert the shell, which looked like a fat overgrown .45 round. Close the breach by raising the stock until it clicked. Fire.

His first two rounds were perfect. Smooth and practiced. Just a couple of seconds between rounds. The grenades exploded high in the trees and spread their tiny pieces of death on everything beneath them behind the mound. I was in good hands.

On his third round, he pointed the weapon toward the top of the trees and opened the breach, but in order to insert the round, he didn't lower the barrel toward the trees above the mound. He kept the barrel pointed almost straight up, inserted the round into the chamber, and raised the stock until it clicked closed. He fired. The round hit the trees directly above our heads, and I took a piece of shrapnel in the chin.

More cuss words with blood seeping out of my chin.

I remember his reply. "Oops. Sorry, Sarge." And he kept firing.

At that point, I began calling my men forward to take and secure the mound. Randal had gotten his act together, and nobody was going to jump up behind that mound and shoot at us for the moment. We had to take that mound.

I think he was a general, but he might have been a colonel. He and the captain came up on my left and ordered us to fall back. I don't remember the exact cuss words I used on him, but I do remember the captain wanting to court-martial me on the spot, but the general/colonel just pulled him away and they disappeared. I obeyed the order. What an incredibly stupid move. That mound would have given us a superior position into the southern entrance to the village. I don't know if we lost any more men taking that mound.

I think that rocket started that two-day battle.

My squad fell back, and we started seeing Huey gunships flying over the river and, with their rockets, raising the temperature to the boiling point. A Huey would descend from the air to unload its entire rocket arsenal into the water, then pull up just as the next stream of rockets screamed passed directly under the rear rotator blades on their tail wing. Later, I began to realize why those officers had pulled us back. They didn't want to lose any more men by taking one mound at a time. They wanted to completely cut the enemy off from any outside support, so our artillery could bombard and decimate them until they had nothing left to fight with. If the enemy tried to escape by jumping into the river, the water would boil them to death. We didn't want them to get away. My apologies to those officers for my cuss words directed toward their persons.

Some of my squad members were given to another squad while the medic looked at my wounds. He laughed at the chin event. Tiny pieces of shrapnel had penetrated the backs of both of my legs. Where had those pieces come from? They had bounced off the soldier behind me. The medic bandaged me up and told me to head toward the chopper pick-up area. I refused to go. Not enough sergeants, and I wasn't wounded that badly. And we were just going to be here for the morning, right? He gave me some pain pills and moved on to the next wounded soldier.

The battle was hot and furious. Everybody was killing the enemy on all fronts. The enemy was shooting rocket after rocket at every one of our positions. We began to yell at them, "Do I look like a tank?! Use a bullet!" Cuss words filled the air.

When I found my E-6 and told him what happened, I told him that I wanted to regroup my squad. A number had already died in another skirmish since the time we had been ordered to retreat from the ditch. I got the rest back.

The killing lulled. We reconsolidated our positions. Movement was a bit difficult with the bandages on my legs. I felt a pain in my right elbow. Along with my legs, a piece had found its way into my elbow as well. It wasn't bleeding. My chin hurt.

At one point, Jeremiah went to pick up an ammo box for his M60. His size had its drawbacks. He made an easy target from a long way off. When he reached down to pick up the ammo box, a rocket went right over his back. He stood up and asked, "Wha' wa' dat?"

I shoved him to the ground and, kneeling over him, kept yelling at him, "You will not die on my watch!"

He laid there whimpering, "Sorry, Sarge."

I yelled, "You will crawl, everywhere!"

"Yes, Sarge."

It was getting dark, but still clear enough to see someone

standing up. The enemy never stood up.

I think the officers were at an impasse as to how to take the village with the fewest number of casualties. Wayne was still alive, although I had no idea how his squad was doing.

My squad had been ordered to move along the tree line opposite the village and cover the rice paddy. Then we were called back to our previous corner. It was about seven in the evening. I don't think anyone had eaten since breakfast. Then the captain ordered my men back toward the center of the tree line. He wanted me to take them along the same path as before. Yes, the enemy knew where we were, but exposing my men to the enemy along the same path, in the open with few trees for cover, while it was still daylight, simply demonstrated that this officer had never seriously been on patrol. Maybe he was trying to impress a superior.

The radioman, with the radio strapped to his back, was standing right next to the captain with the radio's six-foot antenna pointing straight up toward the sky screaming, "Here we are! Shoot us!" The officers needed the radioman close by. Near enough for both of them to get blown up by the same rocket, or at least shoot the person next to the radioman, which was almost always an officer.

I had to lead my squad directly past them. Then the captain ordered me to stop my men right next to him and his antenna.

Where's the line between blind obedience to an order in combat and counting on past experience, intuition, good common sense, and gut feeling? I grant that I probably should have been court-marshaled. That didn't happen.

I stopped just as I passed the captain. I moved about six feet away from him away from the tree line, and I turned around and squatted down on my thighs facing the direction of my men behind me. I ordered the next man to keep moving toward the middle of the tree line where there was better cover and away from the radioman and the captain.

As I waved the third man past, the captain said, "Sergeant, I told you to hold them up!"

I replied, "Yes, Sir!" And I kept waving the men past.

Chain of command. If a sergeant orders a private to do something, and a captain comes along and negates that sergeant's order, the private is still under the sergeant's order until the captain removes the sergeant by giving a direct order to the private. Did that make sense?

I kept quietly yelling to my men, "Move! Keep moving!"

The captain turned around a second time and said, "Sergeant, didn't I give you an order to halt your squad here?"

I replied, "Yes, Sir! You did, Sir!" I waved the next man past.

The captain was still standing next to his radioman. I still had three guys to get past the target antenna and into better cover. I was still squatted down facing those last three men. They had shifted closer to my position away from the captain and his radioman.

Something in front of me shoved me on the left shoulder. No one was in front of me. My men were two to three feet away from me when each one passed me. The shove wasn't a hit, but if I had not reacted to it, I would have fallen backwards on my backside onto the ground. As I was falling backwards, I pushed myself up from my squatting position, lifted my left foot off the ground, pivoted on my right foot to turn me in the direction of my fall, brought my left foot around and took one step with my left foot to regain my balance.

The shock of the pain was probably worse, but the pain went through the roof. The thought went through my head, "Somebody just hit me in the back of the legs with a baseball bat!" I fell flat on my face.

I began yelling for Jeremiah to shoot somebody. I vaguely remember him yelling back, "There's nobody to shoot, Sarge! No one is charging us. We're not under attack! It was a rocket!"

Then I remember the captain coming over and saying with some surprise, "Schneider, have you been wounded again today?" I will not repeat the new title that always surfaces in my mind when I think of him and that question.

What happened? Remember Jeremiah bending down and that rocket flying over his back, but he wasn't hurt? I'm not going into a technical explanation of how rockets work. I'm just describing what others told me what happened to me.

Apparently, when a rocket hits the ground (instead of hitting a standing target) and explodes, the metal flies forward in a pattern of an arc or cone of some degrees (30 degrees? 45 degrees?). People inside that cone are hit, and those outside the cone can't hear for a few minutes afterwards. The metal also seems to stay within a confined channel about four inches in depth/height. And because it hit the ground and exploded, it bounced up and formed that four-inch cone a couple of feet off the ground.

The cluster-f*** formed by that captain had invited a rocket into our midst. It struck the ground just as I had taken my first step, and I was just inside the cone. Dozens of tiny pieces of shrapnel slammed into the back of both legs, and thus my thought about a baseball bat.

Medics were all over it. Another Medevac chopper was called in. They weren't readily available. Another firefight broke out. More people died.

Adrenaline is a marvelous thing. Too bad we can't bottle it without getting addicted to it. I somehow managed to rise up to a crawling position. My E-6 showed up, lifted me to a standing position and moved me away from the open firing line. He helped me strip down to my undershorts and boots. He bandaged both legs to stop the bleeding without cutting off the circulation. He handed me a plastic bag and told me to put all my personal stuff in it. I tossed my wallet and the book I had been reading into the bag. I kept the book in a side pocket in my Army pants. I pulled the book out of my pocket, and it was soaked in blood, my blood. Only the last three chapters were readable. I had read all but those last three chapters. The title of the book was *In Cold Blood*, by Truman Capote. I ripped those three chapters out and stuffed them in the bag with my wallet. I kept my web belt with a couple of M16 magazines on it. I wish someone could have used their iPhone to take a picture of that: butt-naked except for undershorts and boots, a plastic bag, an M16 and a web belt with ammo.

As the E-6 was finishing up, it dawned on me. A couple of things dawned on me. There was no way they would let me stay and continue to lead my men, even if they were short of E-5s who had been in combat longer than ten minutes. After the adrenaline wore off, I wouldn't even be able to stand up. And I hadn't even thought about how long it would take for my legs to heal. I had no choice but to leave the field. Well, the captain didn't need me. He never listened to his experienced sergeants, anyway.

My next thought was revolutionary. "Hey, Sarge, don't they ship you out of Nam if you end up with two Purple Hearts?"

He nodded and frowned.

"Well, I got one on my twentieth birthday and two today."

Actually, I ended up with three Purple Hearts that day. Somebody reported my chin wound as a separate wound, and the Army gave me a Purple Heart for friendly fire. Thanks, Randal.

"I'm going home!" I squealed.

I can't describe Sarge's look. He replied, "You want to leave?"

I didn't understand his question. It wasn't a question. It was a statement.

"Man, I love killing!" he said.

I said nothing. I just stared. I had a lot to thank him for. He had taught me some things in the field that had helped keep me and my men alive. But as I looked at him and heard those words, I thought, "I would rather be dead than be like him."

I'm sure that I could philosophize here on the inherent evil within human nature, but anyone who believes that man is basically good has never read the history books of the last five thousand years. I have one life to live on this earth, and personal combat has been a part of that life. If this is the only life I have, if there is no future life after death, then I need to change my reasons for my self-control and take everything I can get, without getting caught, of course. And if this is the only life I get, then it's BS to claim that my life is going to make an impact for the future generations, who are going to die and go into non-existence, just like me. I am very much looking forward to the next part of my eternal existence that has been arranged for me after I leave this one. For those who have the hope promised by Jesus, who rose from the dead, death is just a door.

The Medevac showed up. I never had time to say goodbye to anyone, not even Wayne. Another barrage of gunfire broke out, and the pilot wanted out of there. I was becoming less mobile, but I was still walking. I loaded last, after the stretchers with my more severely wounded men from my squad.

We left. By the time we reached the field hospital, the adrenaline had gone home, and I couldn't walk anymore. They placed me on a stretcher next to two of my guys. They grabbed one right away and hauled him off to a doctor. They kept going past the guy right next to me.

I kept screaming, "Take him first! I'm fine. He needs help now!"

He died right next to me. In my anguish, I didn't realize what they knew. He was too far gone for help. I had started out with fourteen nameless men in my squad that morning. I lost eleven that day. Three of us, severely wounded, made it out of that battle alive.

They had given me some pain pills, so I was wide awake when they took me into surgery. The doctor smiled at me and asked me something, then stuck a needle into my lower spine. I hardly felt it, probably because of the pain pills. After a few minutes, my legs went completely numb. He took out as much of the shrapnel as he could, then he sewed me back up. I'm sure he used surgical line to do so, but it felt like chicken wire. Once the pain pills wore off, navigating the toilet seat sent streaks of instant pain through my legs. I wondered if I couldn't just stay constipated until they took out the stitches. Why couldn't they just hook up a hose and drain me that way? Because it was a field hospital, Idiot. I had to walk to an outdoor toilet set up for anybody to use. I waited in line once. I hobbled in, turned around, and then tried to figure out how to sit down without letting those chicken wires stab into my wounds. The line grew outside as I gingerly cleaned myself up after each episode.

They kept me in the field hospital for a while before shipping me back to the States. I have no idea why.

The pain pills worked (except for when I had to encounter the tormenting toilet), and I was able to listen to a variety of stories from wounded men who ended up in the field hospital.

One guy had shot himself in the foot with his own .22 pistol, and then claimed that he'd been shot by the enemy. He had become convinced that he would be killed on his next patrol. It's difficult to conceal the wound of a .22 caliber, and his action constituted a court-marshal offense.

Another guy did the same thing, but he said that he didn't care about being court-marshaled. He preferred being alive in prison for a while instead of being dead on the battle field. That guy was asleep when a colonel or general came through the hospital and gave everyone on that ward medals for bravery in combat. Nobody in that ward begrudged that soldier getting a medal. Most everyone thought that it was hilarious. They said that the medal probably got him a lighter sentence.

I finally managed to learn what had happened during my last battle that had replaced our planned R&R week. We had been clueless as to any enemy activity as we descended on that village. Concealment wins in a jungle war. Our INTEL units were providentially blessed that day. They had pinpointed a larger than normal activity in that area, and our unit, overworked and eager for R&R, was the closest one to that village. The assignment: just go take a look, then go SCUBA diving off the coast of Australia.

An unconfirmed report reached us that our company of 220 men had trapped over 600 hardened, battle-experienced

North Vietnamese Army Regulars (NVA) in that village. That's why we spent two days killing each other.

Early the next morning, after I was evacuated from that battle, the NVA had tried to break through our defenses by attacking one of the two corners of the two tree lines. They thought that a corner seemed to be our weakest point. The enemy had attempted to sprint across the long open rice paddy to demolish the corner and break through our lines. The enemy outnumbered us three to one. Had they succeeded, they would have outflanked our entire unit.

Jeremiah and Johnson had been placed on that corner. The report that the sergeant heard from other wounded was that Jeremiah had started firing in short bursts of six to nine rounds, in order to not overheat the barrel of the M60, but the enemy came so fast like a V-shaped wave directly toward his position, that they almost overwhelmed him. He had no choice but to keep up a steady fire with no pauses. Five hundred rounds a minute nonstop. His barrel began to melt.

It's easy enough to replace a barrel. You flick a switch, take the melted one out, pop in the new one, and keep firing. It takes just a second or two. Two problems confronted Jeremiah with the simplicity of this action. First, he needed to have another barrel handy. Johnson carried one extra barrel, and somebody else in the squad carried a third one. Second, Johnson needed a few extra seconds to get the barrel to Jeremiah, so he could swap it out and keep firing. The enemy didn't want to give him those few seconds.

I almost, almost, wish that I had been there to see Jeremiah and Johnson operate. I was told that he went through all three barrels and stacked up sixty bodies directly in front of his position before the enemy realized that their tactic wasn't working. Jeremiah had had no time to change barrels until the melting barrels forced him to do so.

I can visualize it. When Jeremiah realized that he was going to melt down a barrel, he began yelling for a replacement barrel. I can see Johnson pausing ever so quickly from snapping another hundred-round clip onto the one that is charging through the M60 magazine, and hand Jeremiah a spare barrel. Jeremiah glancing to his left, stops firing, pops the melted barrel out, grabs the spare barrel just as Johnson lets go of it, snaps it into the M60, and resumes firing, all within a couple of seconds.

I can hear Johnson yelling for more ammo. I can see a couple of GIs, pausing a second from firing their own weapons to throw into the air those skull-crushing heavy metal boxes of 1,500 rounds of ammo from different directions toward Johnson's voice. Johnson ducks his head down in hopes that those steel boxes, filled with killing bullets, don't kill him by taking his head off. He hopes that they will land close enough to grab and open almost at the same time, so he can keep loading Jeremiah's M60.

Then I can hear Jeremiah yelling for another replacement barrel. Johnson relays the yell to the other men, and now a replacement barrel has been added to the objects flying in Johnson's direction. All coming from different directions and thrown by men who are doing double-duty of scarcely pausing to fire their own weapons while launching ammo and that barrel into the air.

Again, I can see him handing it to Jeremiah, and then returning to snapping together another belt of ammo that is feeding into Jeremiah's M60. Again, Jeremiah glances to his left, stops firing, pops the melted barrel out, grabs the spare barrel just as Johnson lets go of it, snaps it into the M60, and resumes firing, all within a couple of seconds.

Jeremiah melted down two barrels in that firefight. No more barrels. Had the enemy kept coming, Jeremiah and Johnson would have died, and the enemy would have outflanked our entire company. We won that battle. Rumor made it back to me that Jeremiah was going to receive a Silver Star for that action. I hope Jeremiah and Johnson made it home alive. I never knew their first names, and I never saw them again.

The Army eventually shipped me out, lying down on a stretcher. Pumped with pain pills, I woke up in Japan. When they transferred me from one transport aircraft to another one, I received a shock. By sheer coincidence, Nancy was the nurse who grabbed my stretcher.

"Floyd? Is that you?"

I don't remember what I said, but if I had been more conscious, I might have asked her to marry me.

As she passed me off to the next person, she said, "Floyd, please don't go back to Vietnam. You've done enough. I don't want you to come back in a body-bag." Can a person be deeply in love when heavily sedated? I never saw her again.

I woke up when we landed somewhere, and they informed me that we were refueling in Alaska. Then I woke up in San Francisco. Somewhere along the line someone asked me where in the States I wanted to recuperate, and I answered, "My Mom lives in Longmont, Colorado. Plant me at Fitzsimons General Hospital in Denver." That would make it easy for Mom to come visit me, since she and Bill had moved to Longmont by then. Someone related the information to me that the wounded from Vietnam had overwhelmed Fitzsimons' capacity. I woke up in the military hospital in Fort Carson, Colorado.

I've tried to remember the first time I recalled that shove just before the rocket exploded almost right next to me. I have since examined those four-inch scars on the back of both legs and wondered about the position of my body just before something shoved me to stand up. In a standing position, I can still place my hand behind me in the air at the level of those scars, then keeping my hand in place, turn around and bend down to my squatted position on that day. I'm looking directly at my hand at eye-level. Like the soldier who had died earlier that day, that rocket would have taken my head off.

I still have no natural explanation for it. I would like to thank Whomever shoved me.

Wayne was still alive when I left Vietnam. Middle of May, 1968. My first time overseas, and I had spent five months in Vietnam, three and a half months of that time in combat.

9. May - Fall, 1968: Healing

Upon arrival, I was sleeping while they deposited me in a Ft. Carson base hospital bed. I woke up at two in the morning. I froze. I was lying on my back with my knees in the air. An odd position in combat in the jungle. I spread out my fingers and slowly began sweeping my arms away from my body.

Then I heard a soft voice. "Sarge, you're home, in Colorado. You're not in Vietnam. You don't have a weapon. You're safe. Go back to sleep."

I remembered. I think I mumbled, "Thanks."

Three wounded guys had arrived a few weeks earlier, and with nothing to do during the day, they slept, but stayed awake all night playing uninterrupted poker.

I recall as clear as crystal some of the things that occurred during my first week back in the States in that hospital. The cleanliness of the beds and the floors and the medicine tables stunned me. And the nurses dressed in bright white uniforms. I had climbed out of a mud-soaked, germ-infested, disorganized field hospital, where the medics, nurses, and doctors lived under the endless pressure of providing their patients with the absolutely minimum necessities before another patient forced them to move on. And C-Rations. I had entered a world of sparkling white floors, disinfectant tissues, check-ups on the clock accompanied by meticulous reading of charts and nice-looking nurses who usually had time to chat. Oh, and regular delicious meals.

Jet lag kept waking me up before the sun came up. I lay there and listened to the chit-chat and jokes of the three guys in their poker games. They weren't in combat any more. They were living a more civilized life of peace time. The more I adjusted to their conversations, the more I recognized the contrast between their ragging on each other and their discussions of other people, as opposed to the black humor that permeated every second of every waking hour in combat.

Death and suffering and death and pain and death. Fifty years later, I shudder at the things I said about other people's pain and suffering and death while on the battlefield. My mind had existed in a state of constant nervousness: will I die today? Since I might not see tomorrow, I didn't have to be politically correct. Why did I care if I hurt someone's feelings if I was going to die soon? No one was exempt from using black humor, not even the officers. That black humor helped us manage the fear of experiencing those things ourselves. It's crazy to realize that black humor was the only thing that made us laugh at times. The human soul is so resilient and wants so much to survive, that it will resort to the vilest things to cope. I can still be very sarcastic, usually to the damage of others, and to make myself feel good, but God has beaten some of that out of me over the years. I'm glad that my wife and sons never knew me when I was in Vietnam.

Mom showed up that first morning. I lay in bed with both knees bent toward the ceiling and both legs bandaged with gauze and sutures that still felt like chicken wire. More white gauze covered my back and chest. I think I even had bandaids on my elbow and chin. I had needles sticking in my arms, and I'm sure I looked like I had been all shot to pieces.

She came gliding in like a chirpy bird looking for a landing place. She brought light with her. She made everyone smile. We talked. I told her that I didn't have to return to Vietnam, that as soon as my legs got better, I could come home for rehabilitation. She never cried. She spoke to me like an old friend, then like a concerned mother: Are they feeding me well? Are they friendly? Are they changing my dressing often enough?

She came every day to see me. She brought sweets to the guys next to me, if the nurses allowed her to do so, or if they weren't watching. She was always perky.

She chatted with the guys and teased them about cheating each other. She told them to stay away from me. No, she wasn't afraid that they would take my money in a crooked poker game. I had confessed to her that I had learned how to deal from the bottom of the deck at Boy Scout Camp when I was in high school. Mom was afraid that I would take all their money. They adored her. They mumbled some things about being a bit jealous.

I chuckled. "Yeh, I'm blessed," I replied. She was my Mom. I was her only son.

She stayed each time as long as she could. Bill, my stepdad, was actively moving houses (he was a house-mover), and he needed Mom to help get the permits and flag for him on the roads and other details. He had a boatload of work, but he only hired his own sons for his jobs. Mom served as his go-to person for everything else. She loved helping him. It beat waitress work. Marrying Bill had removed her from the poverty line she had lived under all of her eighteen years of married life with Dad. Even in poverty, she had been taking care of people her whole life. I loved Bill for taking such good care of her. She deserved him. Thank you, Jesus, for taking care of my Mom. Now she was taking care of me, again.

Months after I got out of the military, Bill confessed to me what Mom had been like while I was in Vietnam. He would have to ask her a question four or five times before she heard him. She had turned into a zombie. When she came to visit me the first time, the nurse told Bill that she had stood outside the door to my ward and cried and cried. She had to go into the bathroom to clean up her face, so I wouldn't recognize her tears. Some time after getting out of the military and returning home, I accused her of loving me more than Bill. She just put her finger to her lips, like "don't give away our secret," and her eyes twinkled. Bill wouldn't have minded.

Randal showed up one day. He had been wounded soon after me and chose Fort Carson as his hospital. I had given him my Gerber™ knife to keep for me. I had never had to use it in combat. A blessing. He brought it with him to show me that he still had it and would I mind if he held on to it for a while longer. I had no intention of ever using it for its intended purpose. He was a good man. He never brought it back. I never missed it.

I don't remember the normal pain that comes with healing, but eventually I was allowed off base. My first time out I went to see John Wayne in the movie, *The Green Beret*. I walked out feeling no emotion whatsoever. I wondered if I needed counseling for my complete lack of emotion. Counseling sessions? Too inconvenient. I wanted to get on with life. If I didn't talk about the emotional void, then no one would offer me counseling.

Before I was allowed to return home for the rest of my recuperation, I spent my days wandering around Colorado Springs, a twenty-minute bus ride from the base. I finally motivated myself to call Diane in Tennessee. I found the number of the hospital where I thought she worked as a nurse. I found an outside phone booth that wasn't a complete booth. It had three plastics sides and a phone hung on a pole. I called and spoke with the nurse on duty. I asked her if I could have Diane's home phone number. She said that Diane was just around the corner and called her to the phone. Diane was ecstatic that I had made it out alive and was getting better. I mentioned that I was glad to have reached her on duty at work.

"Oh, I'm not on duty," she replied. "This is my day off."

"Then what are you doing at work?"

"Oh, you haven't heard?"

"Heard what?"

"About Wayne."

"What about Wayne?"

"He got wounded."

"Not dead!?"

"Oh, no! He's healing fine." She paused. "He won't be jumping out of any more planes, though."

"Diane, stop keeping me in suspense!"

"The guy in front of him tripped a bouncing betty."

A bouncing betty. The Vietcong had hidden a bomb near a well-travelled trail, rigged it with a pin, that when pulled out, would activate the bomb. A long thin wire connected the pin to a small almost invisible stake on the other side of the path. If a soldier wasn't paying close attention to his every step, he might step over it, or he might trip it. Once the bomb was clicked, some kind of mechanism shot the bomb a few feet into the air, where it exploded in all directions showering everyone close by with shrapnel.

Diane continued. "Wayne heard the click, the soldier who tripped the wire fell flat on his face. Wayne dropped into a crouch and turned his body ninety degrees to the right to offer as little area of his body as possible, while pulling his helmet down over the left side of his head to protect his eyes and ear and chin. The blast knocked him down, one piece of shrapnel went straight through his left knee, but it didn't hit any nerves."

I remember yelling for joy so loudly, that people across the street looked like they were going to call the police. So Wayne couldn't jump out of planes any more. He was alive, and he would heal fine.

"But that's not all," she continued.

How much better could it get?

"He agreed with you and me that Jesus makes more sense than anything else, so he has chosen to follow Jesus also."

I began to tingle. Every pore of my body oozed euphoria. I almost dropped the phone from dancing around inside the almost-phone booth. I was yelling again, like I had just won a major battle.

I didn't manage to see Wayne again until I was mustered out in March, 1969. The Army stationed him in Louisiana. I drove through, and we spent an afternoon watching him beat another guy playing Monopoly.

I spent a couple months at home. Mom and I were connected at the hip. We bought material for her sewing projects and books for my reading addiction. We ran errands for Bill, and, at some point, she started teaching me how to cook. She confessed that when she had married dad, she didn't know how to boil water. I never fell in love with cooking but hearing Mom's laugh at my mistakes moved me to orchestrate more accidents.

I was sitting out on the porch alone one evening gazing at an indescribable sunset over the Rockies to the west. Mom came out, sat down next to me, and said nothing for a long time.

Then she asked, "Floyd, what do you really want to do with your life?"

When I was ten years old, my parents gave me a chemistry set. Back then the laws allowed a lot more experimental freedom for curious future scientists. Two booklets on atomic energy came with the set. I had read them from cover to cover. I didn't understand everything I read, but those two booklets set me on a course for a PhD in physics. And the University of Colorado in Boulder was famous for drug addicts and nuclear physicists. I was still trying to figure out how I could take a pre-algebra course while I was still in the Army.

I don't know what I had been thinking about, when Mom asked me that question, but those two booklets in chemistry sprang into my mind. And then I thought about all those guys in Vietnam I had talked to about Jesus. And I thought about Wayne.

I have no idea why I said what I said, but I said it.

"If I tell you, you won't laugh?"

Her expression softened more than ever. "No, of course not."

Looking out at the brilliant sunset, I replied, "I think I want to be like Billy Graham."

She paused for just a split second, got up and said, "Then I'll start praying about that for you," and she walked back into the house.

I really wanted to return to my diving buddies in California, but I forgot to terminate my jump status. I ended up being assigned to the 82nd Airborne Division in Fort Bragg, North Carolina, as far away from Carmel as possible.

Bummer.

Mom was her old self again. I wasn't going back into combat. The Army sent me home, and I healed in four months. Mom and I went everywhere together: shopping, movies, helping Bill at work, church, eating out together. Fall arrived, and I needed to finish out my enlistment time. I kissed Mom, told her that I might see her at Christmas, but if not, then in May. I would call on a regular basis. I jumped in my Ford Mustang and drove straight through to Fort Bragg, North Carolina.

10. September – March, 1969: The Final Stretch

I had joined the Army with one of my best friends in high school, Mark. We ended up being stationed at Fort Bragg at the same time. He hadn't been a grunt in Vietnam.

My orders placed me in a new company that the Army had called into existence to form a new Brigade. We had a captain as our company commander, but we didn't have enough officers to lead every platoon yet. My E-7 platoon sergeant treated everyone fairly. He just wanted to climb in rank more. Understandable, if you were a "lifer." When he saw that I had been in combat, he put me in charge of the platoon. Bummer. I spent the first couple of weeks ordering the guys to dig fox holes on maneuvers. We practiced jumping less often than I wanted to. Transported to the airfield, picked up your chute, got in the plane, jumped out, went home. Jumping beat digging fox holes.

Two E-3s in the company office were holding down the clerk positions. They were nervously waiting for orders that would send them to Vietnam. I approached my company sergeant, an E-9, and informed him that I had no intention of re-enlisting, that his two company clerks would be leaving very soon, and that I was extremely tired of digging fox holes, so could I please become the company clerk. He looked at my three stripes and mentioned that combat sergeants weren't trained to be clerks. I replied that a combat sergeant could serve him better than a private in that clerk position, especially since we were forming a new battalion. He pondered my arguments for a second, then looked at his calendar, noted the time and day, and told me to show up at division headquarters for a two-day seminar on how to fill out the Morning Report.

Every morning at 6 a.m. everyone had to stand in line on the parade ground, in formation, ready for roll call. If everyone was there, the company clerk checked the box that everyone was there. If someone was missing, the company clerk checked the box with the missing name. If that person showed up later, which he usually did, he reported to the company clerk who ushered him into the company sergeant's office for explanations and the appropriate reprimand. An E-5 combat sergeant received less flack from the derelicts than a private. I read the over-simplified notes during the first hour of the seminar, and then rested my thoughts from Army matters until I passed the exam the second day. When I handed the certificate to the sergeant, he called in my E-7 to inform him of his loss. My platoon sergeant, though understandably upset, realized that an E-9 outranked an E-7 by a few years.

The operations sergeant, an E-6, got drunk a lot. His assistant, an E-5 from Washington state, was low key, laid back and very organized. The week following my appointment as company clerk, the higher brass informed us that headquarters would be carrying out an AIG (Army Inspecting General) inspection on our company next Monday morning. It was Thursday afternoon. When faced with an AIG inspection, everybody goes berserk. The Army gives you twenty minutes to do something that takes three days. They expect you to fail the inspection, at least the first time, to encourage everyone in the company to work harder and do a better job the next time. Nobody ever said that, but whatever.

Our E-9 gave us the speech, "We're up to this. Let's get it done." The Operation E-5 and I put our heads together. Neither of us had families, we weren't party animals, and we slept in the barracks. We took the E-6 out for a drink on Thursday evening, then another drink, then another drink; then we took him home and asked his wife to keep him there until Monday morning. We told her that we would cover for him on Friday. We didn't tell her about the AIG inspection. She didn't ask any questions.

I still had my two E-3s who had not gone off to Vietnam yet. I don't think we polished the silverware in the mess hall, but we would have done that if necessary. Sleep was not on the agenda.

Monday morning arrived. On the parade ground, uniforms sparkled and weapons, cupped in hands perfectly aligned and angling toward the blue sky, commanded the attention of the inspectors. Drill order resounded sharp and clear. Every speck of dust in the supply office and the company office been ordered out of existence. Trash bins were emptied, and every piece of paper stood at attention in its proper folder. Our company passed with a 94%. The first time. Our E-9 called the two of us into his office after all the brass had left. He asked where the E-6 was and we said, "Busy."

He informed us that he owed us a great debt of gratitude. We both knew that passing that AIG with a 94% the first time gave him a lot of clout with the higher-ups. His humility under those E9 stripes impressed and touched me. I should have learned from his humility sooner, but at least I remember how he connected humility with command.

I had no nightmares from the horrors of combat, but sometimes anger rose inside me from what I considered an incredible waste of young lives. Even though I had only lost some non-friends in Vietnam, I found myself looking for an argument for reasons I couldn't define. I was refining the art of sarcasm, and I didn't care which side of the argument I found myself on. If one of my superiors got something wrong, I waited to see if a spark of humility surfaced. If it didn't, I judged the possible damage to myself if I engaged that person's arrogance, and, if I deemed the damage worth it, I sarcastically pointed out that person's mistake. Needless to say, I was more arrogant than those I engaged, but blindness to one's own sins runs rampant in arrogant people.

One day a second lieutenant came into the office and snarled at my two E-3s. I stepped into the room and asked him if I could be of some help. He snarled at me. I asked him how long he had been out of OCS (Officer Candidate School). The question stunned him, and he stammered why that was any of my business.

I replied, "First, you never learned chain-of-command. Those E-3s are under my command, and if you have a problem with them, you address me, *Sir*. Second, (I pointed to my three stripes on my arm) you obviously can't recognize an E-5 combat veteran whom you should respect because you just got out of the classroom, Sir!"

He went charging into the company commander's office demanding that I be severely reprimanded. Our captain called my E-9 into his office, heard both sides of the story, then excused both myself and the lieutenant for a few minutes while he discussed things with my E-9. The lieutenant was called in first. Less than two minutes later, the lieutenant came out with a terrifying look of shock on his face. I was called in. The captain informed me that I would end up serving time if I ever spoke to another officer like that. He agreed that the lieutenant deserved my comments, but things like that had to go through channels. Enlisted men are not allowed to take things into their own hands. I was blessed with a company commander who was not a tyrant and who was honest enough to admit the failings of younger inexperienced officers.

Before being dismissed, my E-9 took me back into his office for a "chat." He never told me whether he had influenced the captain's decision in any way, but he informed me, off the record, that the captain had immediately transferred the lieutenant to another unit outside of our battalion with no positive or negative reason for the transfer. My E-9 had seldom ever had to give me a direct order, until now. He knew I wasn't going to re-enlist, so when I finished the Morning Report around seven am, he was ordering me off the base for the rest of the day, except for my rotational kitchen duty. Neither of us could stifle a slight smile, as he waved me out of his office. That incident came the closest to damaging me due to my arrogance.

Mark and I spent more time together. He had a Pontiac GTO with a 360-engine, and I had a 1966 Ford Mustang with a V8, 289, that produced 225-horsepower with a 4-barrel carburetor. Red. Bill, my stepdad, had helped me buy it at an auction for $600.00. That's entirely another story.

A long wide road stretched for a long way on one end of the base. Army Regulations allowed no drag races on that road, but the MPs would sit in their vehicles next to the non-drag strip and place bets as to who would win the next race. Mark and I started racing each other and soon discovered that my small 289 was off the line before his GTO even woke up, but when that GTO kicked into full power, in just over a quarter of a mile, he left me in the dust. We finally got pulled over by the MPs and told to stay off their drag strip. We were too predictable.

Mark and I let each other drive each other's car. One weekend, with me in the driver's seat, we drove his GTO into Washington, D.C. I drove around a six-lane round-about, the wrong way, twice, then skedaddled back south to the base. Another long weekend found us, with Mark at the wheel, driving my Mustang all the way to Key West. We pulled just off the road to take a nap on the freeway. A frowning policeman woke us up, but when he discovered that we were with the 82nd Airborne Division and were just enjoying a free weekend, he lightened up. He told us that he held us in high respect (he meant it), but we still couldn't sleep on the freeway.

Cussing

Back in the States I began to notice that I cursed less. I found that odd. Eventually, I realized that culture determines "curse" words. If I'm speaking English with non-German speakers, and I use the words, "verdammt," or "scheisse," a puzzled look will appear on my English-speaking friends' faces. If a German person hears those words, he will respond accordingly as he would to most other German cusswords. The subculture determines the appropriate or inappropriate use of a cuss word. Some Christian subcultures have banned the word "heck" as a violation of Ephesians 4:29 ("foul language") and Ephesians 5:4 ("not fitting"). Back in the early seventies, a friend of mine got a job speaking at a Christian radio station and had to change his last name from "Heck" to "Hunt" while speaking on the air.

I could cuss with the best of them. When I watched the movie, *Platoon*, and heard the F-word three out of four times in a sentence, I recognized myself back then. But I also had learned to love reading at a very young age. When I was ten years old, the local library in Frederick, Colorado, had offered a special gift to any child who would read ten books over the summer. Mom supplemented that gift with her own gift. I don't remember what I received from the library or from Mom, but I remember the joy of reading.

At some point, I realized that when I read a book full of cuss words, I skimmed over them. Why did I do that? Because they didn't take the story any further. They just show the character or emotion of the person doing the speaking. Everybody in a military unit cussed. Even the priests. Well, not everybody. That very rare eccentric who didn't cuss stood out. Others made fun of him. Called him pious names. That's almost funny. Everybody wants to be unique and different. Everybody wants to call their own shots. But if somebody really did that by not cussing, the others couldn't handle it. They somehow felt judged by that non-cussing soldier, so they cussed him out, even if he never treated them as if they were beneath him.

I'm not better than anyone else, and I've been much worse than some. I've done my own fair share of cussing during my life time, and I doubt my cussing days have ended entirely, but I've never made fun of someone who refused to use cuss words. And if I find myself in a subculture that rejects certain words or expressions as foul language, then I do my best to avoid them. Cussing or not cussing doesn't define who I am. It just describes how I'm feeling and how I'm expressing myself at that moment those words come out of my mouth.

Virginity

Mark's schedule was not as open as mine. I was the one who discovered the Christian Servicemen's Center in downtown Fayetteville, NC. I was just driving around, not sure of where I was, and I entered a street with lots of red lights on many of the doors. I had no idea that I had stumbled into the Red Light District, the working home of prostitutes.

I didn't have a lot of friends as a kid. Others made fun of me a lot. I'm not whining; I'm explaining. I've been rejected for just about everything in my life. Being different was dangerous.

When I was a young teenager, Mom told me that I needed to keep that thing in my pants until I was married. I had no idea what she was talking about. I carried a knife in my pants, but I had no idea what that had to do with marriage.

When I was seventeen, I was active in the church youth group, and I was one of the town's life guards over the summer. A very promiscuous female from out of town showed up that summer and wanted to take me to bed. She must have been really desperate, because I never gave any thought to doing more than kissing in the front or back seat. The local high school playboy came along and did her bidding. He never made fun of me. I think he somehow respected me for rejecting her offer.

In Vietnam the "boom-boom girls" cost $1.00. That was the price of a soft drink. Sometimes a boom-boom girl would offer herself to a couple dozen guys in one evening. The men stood in line for their turn. I was never drawn to that, and no one ever made fun of me. Yes, they tried to encourage me to jump in with them, but I had earned their respect in other ways, so I didn't suffer the barrage of sneering criticism and abuse they poured on those who couldn't carry their own weight. Weakness was worse than morality.

So when I stumbled into the Red Light District, it had no effect on me. Something inside told me that I had the right to be different, and when it came to morality, I didn't have to answer to the sex-driven crowd. I didn't have to justify being different in an area that few people really understood. I didn't have to cower when accused of not being able to satisfy my wife in bed on our wedding night because I hadn't had any previous practice.

Then I realized that my choice to be different in this area had given me an experience that very few people had ever had or ever will have. I had chosen to save my sexuality and remain a virgin until I got married. And further, I chose to only marry someone who herself was a virgin. God blessed those decisions.

Back in the States, guys would ridicule me for my decision to not play around. I usually ignored them, but one time has cemented itself into my memory. A couple guys with dates on their arms wanted to set me up with a third girl. They kept pointing out how good she was in bed. The other two girls were snickering. I didn't get mad. I just thought that they were so very shallow.

I responded, "Don't I have the right to be different from most everybody else and make one woman happy? Don't I have the right to put her on a pedestal and treat her like a queen? When you have an affair, you're not thinking of anything but yourself. I will choose to think of my wife. And she will love me more deeply for it." And then I glanced at their two dates. They had shame written all over their faces. I hadn't intended to make the girls feel uncomfortable, but I think they wished that their dates had held them in higher esteem.

I have since told many people that I'm sorry that they are just like everybody else when it comes to sex, and that they will never know what it's like to be able to tell your wife, "I saved it for just you." That usually stops the jeering criticism and the entire conversation. Followers of Jesus never have to cower before the non-different world when Hollywood affairs and sex are thrown in their face. Stand your ground. Be different, seriously.

The Christian Servicemen's Center

I parked in front of a Red Light house and ascended the stairs to find out what a Christian Serviceman's Center was all about. I met Jim Morrison. We talked. He heard my story. He told me his. He had been a Minnesota policeman for eight years, then switched to working with GIs, helping them find purpose in life. His muscles bulged out of his shirt. No one could ever accuse him of being a wimp. He wanted to know if I was reading my Bible regularly. I answered, irregularly. He responded by telling me to get my act together. I never saw him treat someone else the way he treated me. He challenged most everything I said. I now realize that I wore my arrogance on my sleeve, visible to everybody but myself.

Over the first few weeks, it became obvious to him that I was looking to date some girls. Christian girls showed up there to meet Christian GIs. At one point, I walked into the room where he was sitting chatting with a couple of nice young ladies. He looked up, saw me, and said, "Oh, Floyd Schneider. He knows everything. If you don't believe me, just ask him." The girls giggled. And I hadn't even said anything yet. Apparently, I was more obnoxious back then than I am now. That's depressing.

I became a regular visitor. No other guys showed up from my own unit. The ones who did show up said that they were also the only ones in their units who had chosen to follow Jesus. This Center and the local churches offered the only haven for fellowship-starved GIs.

During the week, I worked as a clerk, six to seven-thirty in the morning, then I was off-base. I returned to the base for supper because the food was free and good. Occasionally, I ended up on KP (working in the kitchen), but I rather enjoyed that. The privates had to serve the lieutenants, who tended to be quite arrogant, especially those who had not seen combat. We wished that they would all be sent to Nam. Because I was an E-5, I got to choose what I did on KP. I always chose pot and pans. I washed up all the big kitchen ware toward the back, away from the officers. Most guys didn't like pots and pans, because you were still cleaning up after everyone else had left. In addition to avoiding the officers, I had made friends with the head cook. He liked me because I wasn't lazy. I liked him because he didn't try to boss me around. His specialty was baking. I became his first tester and the last person to clean up any leftovers. The other guys could never figure out why I looked forward to KP duty.

But invariably, every evening after supper, Mark and I would be accosted by the other guys in the barracks to join them in their drinking or drug parties for sex-capades. We weren't prudes. We could joke and cuss as well as anyone, but we just didn't want to go experience the rampant devastation the other men were bringing on themselves. And since the Center wasn't always open, we fled to the drive-in theater. It opened at 6 p.m., the first movie started at 7 p.m., and the fourth movie ended around 4 a.m. During the week, we watched the first and the second and then went back to the barracks. I still had to do the Morning Report and Mark had his own duties. On weekends, we watched the first movie, ate our way through the second one with pizza and soft drinks, slept through the third one and stayed until the fourth was finished. We did that for eight months.

I don't remember Jim's schedule for closing the Serviceman's Center, but I do remember becoming addicted to movies. If the Center closed at 8 p.m., then Mark and I would watch only one movie on weekdays and three on weekends.

After I had been showing up for a number of weeks at the Center, I began to feel comfortable around everyone there. We can never see ourselves as we really are until someone points out a weakness or two. My arrogance was about to take a long-needed hit. I had just arrived at the center one day when Jim approached me, and without any warning, picked me up by my arm (he was really strong), carried me into a back room, sat me down and asked me,

"Are you a follower of Jesus?"

I sputtered, "Yes."

He replied, "Then please, for Jesus' sake, don't tell anybody. You're the worst example of a Christian I've ever met."

Uh, I was stunned. When people tell me I'm crap, I first take into consideration who they are. Does the person dumping on me care about me? Usually no, so I write it off as their problem. But over the weeks, I realized that Jim really cared about me. I had never had someone who cared about me obliterate me that much.

I don't recall the rest of the conversation, but I began reading my Bible more, while still trying to figure out how to get a date.

Toward the end of my enlistment, the Army decided to offer us training in a field of our choice that would provide us with a job once we got out. Mark and I both chose Financial Advising, which would train us to be stock brokers. During one of those seminars, a group of eight guys from a cult aggressively challenged both of us. They came at us from every side. Our view of the Bible was all wrong. They had the truth, and we needed to join them. That afternoon we ran back to Jim begging for answers to their rhetorical questions. They had all the answers, and we were ignorant for not believing what they believed.

He handed me a large Bible concordance and told me I could use it all day long. I just couldn't take it home. I hated him (not really, he was just really irritating, to me, at least). Mark and I spent most of the day looking up and writing down Bible verses and marking them in our Bibles. The next day we caused that group so much consternation, that they took our Bibles away from us and commanded that we answer their questions without the use of our Bibles. We looked at each other and burst out laughing. "We win," and we said no more. I think Mark told them to keep our Bibles if they would read them, in context, of course. We were learning that all the cults take Bible verses out of context to support their views.

After that experience, Jim began giving me more personal advice. He gave personal advice to everyone. Usually he waited until someone asked, but in my case, he didn't wait. I'm certain that he tried to pound a lot of stuff into my brain, but of all the stuff he pushed on me, only two things really stuck.

First, the Bible is the only book God ever wrote. If someone tries to tell you what's in the Bible, ask them, politely, to show you the text, because you can read it for yourself. Then read the entire context, not just one part of one verse. Be polite about it. He kept emphasizing the politeness part of my response.

His second piece of advice, I will never forget. It was just for me: "Until you have died for the sins of trillions of people, you have no right to be bitter about anything. Get over it and move on. God will take care of what other people do that disturbs you." My anger ran deep about Vietnam. I was experiencing an internal war between wanting to hurt someone for that war or letting God dispense the appropriate justice. And even when I relented inside and told Jesus that I knew He could destroy evil people better than I could, I still wanted to be used by Him in the process. Jim had nailed me.

Then he added, "Bitterness only destroys the person who is bitter. Don't forget that. You just have to move on and leave bitterness behind you."

Jim helped me more than he realized. He tried to talk me into going to a Bible college in the area before going off to Boulder for my physics degree. In the first place, he felt that a university might mess with my mind. I laughed at that one. Maybe I was a bit arrogant, but I'd learned to handle attacks toward my faith. Second, he wanted me to go to one close by because he said that I would do well helping him with other military guys. He seemed to think that I had changed enough to be of some use to him and his ministry. I would have loved to stay. Jim was one of the few men I listened to in my life. He cared about me. But when I started looking into Bible college, I wanted to be close to Mom.

My discharge date loomed ever closer. Just four months away. The Army then informed me that they were offering an "Early Out" if you chose to go to college when you left. Only two requirements. Get accepted into the accredited university of your choice, and get the right signatures on the request for an "Early Out."

I navigated the first hurdle in less than two weeks. Since I wanted to be in Colorado, and I wanted to study physics, I chose Colorado State University, CSU, because it was easier to get into for the spring quarter, and it was close enough for weekend visits to Mom who lived south of Littleton. The Army only needed an acceptance letter from the university. They didn't specify any major or care about the courses I signed up for. I signed up for Sport Parachuting, Skiing, SCUBA diving, Tennis, and Pre-calculus. I was going to enjoy my freedom. When I did finally arrive at CSU, for lack of students signing up, they had to drop four of my courses. I ended up just taking Pre-calculus. I joined a Sport Parachuting club off campus. That's another book.

The second condition presented me with a problem. The chain of command. After I filled out the proper forms, and my platoon sergeant had signed them, I had to make an appointment to see an officer at battalion headquarters, then one at brigade level, then one at division level. An officer, anywhere along the way, who had eaten something that had disagreed with him, could disapprove my request simply because he was an officer.

I started low in hopes that the higher ups would just sign off on it. I typed out my reasons, signed a statement stating that I wasn't lying, attached the CSU acceptance letter, and asked the Adjunct Second Lieutenant, Steven N. Tingey, to sign the approval form. He did. So far so good. Then my company commander, Captain Patrick G. Milroy, signed a recommendation approval letter stating that I wasn't a necessity for the performance of the unit's mission and that I was not a criminal. One more step, the Adjutant General (AG), who is the military chief administrative officer. A General? A Colonel? No, when I walked in and asked who should I see about signing my request, the clerk pointed me toward a desk plate that read: Dennin E. Reeves, 2LT, INF, Act Asst AG. I don't even think he looked up when he signed it.

With just a couple weeks left, orders came for our company to perform some training exercises in Jamaica. My E-9 called me in and told me that I was staying behind and not going on the training exercises. Seriously?! The exercises held no thrill for me, but they would only last a couple hours a day. A week in Jamaica on a semi-vacation, and I was stuck at a desk in North Carolina. Before I could cry and whine, he said that he was turning the company over to me to hold down until they returned in a week. Besides, since I was "Short," about to leave within the next two weeks, I was the perfect person for the job. End of discussion.

On the first day of exercises, the reserve pilots were instructed to fly over the jungle and have the troops parachute out the left door, thus landing on the beach. Then the pilots were instructed to turn around and fly over the water and let the rest of the troops parachute out the same left door, thus landing on the beach. The Army was using these exercises to train both pilots and paratroopers.

Somewhere along the line of miscommunication, the pilots flew over the beach, and the troops parachuted out both right and left doors. Nobody hit the beach. Half the troops landed in the trees and the other half went swimming. No casualties. Some injuries and some broken equipment. Someone upstairs called off the rest of the exercises and returned everyone to base in North Carolina.

The next day, when my E-9 came into his office, I was sitting at his desk. He looked at me and said, "Don't even think about saying anything." He wasn't smiling. I choked down a couple of hilarious retorts.

I was discharged less than two weeks later. I came out with the "Award of the Air Medal." The official reason given for this medal was "For meritorious achievement while participating in aerial flight in February, 1968, while serving with Company A, 1st Battalion (Airborne) 502nd Infantry." In plain English, I didn't fall out of any helicopter. I was awarded one "Army Commendation Medal with V (Valor) Device" for "Heroism in the Republic of Vietnam" on my 20th birthday. I did not wake up that morning planning on being a hero. That birthday also garnered me my first Purple Heart. I got three more in May. My DD-214 reads "Purple Heart (3 OLC)," which means three Oak Leaf Clusters, each one being an individual Purple Heart. I think that I just kept standing up at the wrong time. On March 17, 1969, I was transferred to inactive status of the Army Reserve, which meant that I didn't have to pull any more duty. The Army paid me for 19 days leave that I had not used before being discharged. That almost seemed like a crime, since for the last eight months I spent so much time off the base anyway. I would use the money for gas to drive home to Mom.

11. March, 1969: Out

My Army career ended in March, 1969, with no ceremony. A lieutenant handed me my discharge papers and wished me well. I said goodbye to Mark and Jim Morrison and mumbled that we should stay in contact. We didn't. I drove southwest from North Carolina to Louisiana to see Wayne for a couple of hours. He told me that he was jealous that I had gotten out before him. I told him that I was jealous that he had a wife like Diane. We hugged and separated.

As I left Wayne, I plugged in a tape cassette and began playing and singing, "My Jesus, I Love Thee." I saw no reason for me to still be alive. The first two lines of the third stanza of that song stuck in my brain: "I'll love Thee in life, I will love Thee in death," followed by the second line, "And praise Thee as long as Thou lendest me breath." I have a love for music that borders on extreme eclecticism, from Rock and Roll to Classical Operettas, but I still love that song the most.

Why had Jesus spared me? I've long since discovered that He seldom answers those questions. He expects me to make decisions based on His instructions, trust Him to close any doors He doesn't want me walking through, and to leave the future in His hands. I will just keep praising Him as long as He gives me breath do to so.

So now what?

Eventually, Vietnam faded out of my memory, and I saw no reason to dwell on the past. I couldn't change it. My wounds had healed, and the only thing that forced the memories above consciousness were those tiny pieces of metal that kept popping out of my elbow, chin and the back of my thighs for years. I was told that even the body protects itself by rejecting foreign objects. It seemed ironic that my physical body was attempting to do for me physically what my mind was going to do for me emotionally. Both succeeded. I quickly discovered that I could talk openly about my combat experiences without any remorse or recurring nightmares. On the way to Colorado, I stopped to visit an old high school friend. He asked me if it bothered me to talk about Nam. When I said no, he took me to an indoor public swimming pool and showed my scars to all the girls. I didn't have time to hang around for any dates.

As I crossed the Colorado State Line, I continued wondering what kind of party Mom was planning for my return home. It wouldn't be extravagant. Mom's antics could turn a large boring party into something unforgettable for anybody courageous enough to show up, but Mom loved people one at a time.

Mom threw a private party for just the two of us when I arrived home. I was the lone recipient of her love at this party. She then talked me into getting my real estate license (which I've always kept active anytime I was in the States). She saw no incongruity with her "Billy Graham" paying his own way through life by selling real estate.

It takes time to gain enough clients in real estate before a person begins to make a decent wage, so I picked up a part-time job as a security guard and applied to become a deputy sheriff for Jefferson County, Colorado. The Sheriff called me and his sad voice informed me that the position required a minimum age of 23, but would I seriously think about applying again in two years. He wanted guys with military experience on his team.

The police officer who owned the security guard company gave me a squad car and night duty. I was single. The other guards wanted to spend time with their families. A bar owner had problems closing at 2 in the morning. When I cleaned up that problem, he offered me a full-time job, which I turned down, and my boss gave me a small raise. Another business owner had marriage problems, got drunk and chose to sleep in his business office one night. He forgot to turn off his security alarm, which went off when he turned over in his sleep in the middle of the night. He woke up from a dead sleep to hear me yelling for him to come out with his hands up. When he looked out the window, my patrol car lights blinded him. He stumbled out the door and found himself looking down the barrel of a handgun held by a very serious security guard. He immediately threw his hands straight into the air and began screaming, "Don't shoot! I'm the owner!" When he sobered up, he gave my boss a small bonus for the company's efficiency. I got part of that bonus.

Boredom began creeping into my psyche. I joined a Sport Parachute club. I was the only Vet, but I was still the novice. They had to teach me to pack my own chute. I had stumbled into a bunch of well-educated agnostics. We all loved being belligerent and sarcastic, and we argued about everything philosophical and religious. Sometimes we slept in the hanger and one time three of us argued until four in the morning while they kept making me practice packing and repacking my parachute.

We never broke the protocol for jumping. Nobody broke the rules. Things still happened, but nobody broke the rules. On every jump, we checked and rechecked each others' equipment. That saved the life of our jump master once.

We jumped everywhere from Littleton to Gunnison (windy!). In Gunnison, four of us went up together with a pilot who had served in Vietnam. We were all four novices. We had each jumped out five times with the static line, and now we were allowed to jump out at something like 3,000 feet above the ground, I think (that was a long time ago) and pull our own rip cord. I began talking with the pilot about our Nam experiences while the other three jumped out.

He looked at his altimeter and told me it was my turn. I didn't look at the altimeter. I jumped out and immediately pulled my rip cord. After I looked up to see that beautiful white circle saving me from certain death, I looked around at the mountains and the high desert. Then I looked down. Oops. I had jumped out at 6,000 feet. The wind loved those kinds of mistakes. It used the extra 3,000 feet to carry me miles away from the DZ (drop zone) and deposit me among the cacti and rattlesnakes. The jump club had to send a jeep to retrieve me. I was reprimanded, rightly so, but the pilot kept saying that he thought I had more experience than a novice since I had been in the Airborne. They informed him that paratroopers always jumped out at 1,000 feet with a static line, and next time he needed to keep track of who was jumping out of his plane.

They were just ticked off that they had to send a jeep to track my descent and save me from carrying my chute five miles back to the DZ. I was the one who had the funniest story to tell at the party that night. Each time I told the story, it got better. At first telling, I had to avoid a huge cactus. At second telling, a fence showed up in the story. Eventually, a herd of rattlesnakes were nipping at my boot laces. I think the club members liked my stories even more because I was the only one who didn't get drunk at the party. I drove our club members back to the motel in the early morning for our return trip back to the Eastern Slope in the late morning.

The security job and jumping out of planes failed to suffocate the insidious boredom lurking just beneath my consciousness. I had to admit that, after being submerged for three years in the military culture, I missed parts of the Army. My body probably missed the adrenalin.

I walked into the National Guard office and asked the sergeant what reasons he could give me to sign up. He informed me that the Army was giving a new test to everyone, so could I please take the test first, and then come back tomorrow after the test had been graded. I took the test.

That was the dumbest test ever. There were only two answers to every question. If you answered A, you were the most naive person on the planet. If you answered B, you had knowledge of every perversion man had ever developed. I put down all A's. When I returned the next day, a Colonel wanted to speak with me. He told me that this test was a character test, and that my score had gone through the roof. He had read my record and asked me what the Army could offer me to entice me to re-enlist. That was different. I flippantly said that I wanted the Army to pay for my bachelor degree in physics, and then I wanted to be assigned to the DLI, Defense Language Institute, in Monterey, CA, to study Hebrew. Jim Morrison had impressed on me how important the biblical languages of Hebrew and Greek were. So I though I would start with the oldest one first.

As I was speaking, the Colonel was writing furiously on a piece of paper. When I finished, he slid that piece of paper across the table to me and said, "Sign here."

Whoa! Wait a minute. I replied, "Let me guess. I'll get all I've asked for, but I'll end up in Jerusalem in Intelligence."

He nodded.

What an offer! Something inside said no. I declined. His head sank onto his chest, and I went to Bible college in the fall.

Ready for a new adventure, I entered the surreal world of Bible college that assaulted me with the polar opposites of an invaluable education that penetrated and analyzed the most important issues in life, and a world of semi-extreme legalism. Going to a movie was almost a capital offense. One movie and they kicked you out of Bible college. A guy and a gal couldn't be in the same room together alone, not even a brother and sister. The Ladies' Dorm Mother measured the female students' skirt lengths.

In November, I attended the school's mandatory Missions Conference. A mission's representative, Don Bruggman, gave a spiel on Greater European Mission (GEM). That intrigued me. When I asked a couple of questions, he tried to talk me into joining their France team for the summer missions trip.

I informed him that my last name was Schneider, and that I would consider going to Germany, but not France. He said that the German team was already full. I reminded him that I was paying for my entire trip. He allowed the German team to take an extra person for the summer.

I'm not sure how much that missions trip had anything to do with missions. It certainly had nothing to do with evangelism. We ended up being used as manual labor to rebuild the second story of a castle into class rooms. We picked cherries and ran errands for those who lived there full time.

I met Clarence and Jim. The US Draft had allowed Clarence, as a Mennonite Conscientious-Objector, to spend two years working with GEM in Germany. He had arrived a year ahead of me. Jim had just graduated from the Reserve Officer Training Corp (ROTC) program at Wheaton. He had been given this summer to do whatever he wanted before entering the Army as a second lieutenant and being sent to Vietnam as a combat officer. He was such a nice guy, and extremely knowledgeable about everything. I told him very few stories about officers in Nam. I attempted to read *Escape From Reason*, by Francis Schaeffer and got lost on the first page. Jim took me through that book, word-by-word. I'm sure I used up most of his patience in this lifetime. When the summer ended, and we separated, we never connected again. He would receive orders to go to Vietnam as a second lieutenant. I think the thought hovered on the lower edge of my consciousness that Jim was one of those whose first names I didn't want to know.

The last week of that trip changed my life and sent me in a completely different direction. Although I had fallen in love with one of the other summer interns, Cherie, she wasn't interested in dating, since she didn't believe that we would ever see each other again after the summer was over.

During the last week of that summer, the staff gave us plebeians three free days in Regensberg. We slept in a youth hostel inside the old part of the city, the castle part. On the first afternoon, I walked out of the castle gate with the intention of strolling around the wall to the next gate and reentering the city. Uh, there's only one gate built into a castle. By the time I had walked around the entire old city, it was 5 p.m., and I was really ticked off at myself. Against GEM policy, I walked into a bar and ordered a cola. I noticed five very happy, almost-drunk Germans sitting together nursing their beers. I'm always open for new experiences. I reached into my back pocket, pulled out a small German New Testament, walked over to the table and asked them if I could share something with them. In German, of course. They agreed to let me speak.

I got about three sentences out when one of them yelled at me (in German), "Why are you bringing this crap to us here in Germany! Take it back to America where you got it!"

I replied, "Hey, hold on! I tell people about Jesus anywhere I go."

To which he replied, "Oh! Well in that case, tell us more."

One of them said, "That cola will rot your gut. Let me buy you a beer."

I thanked him but declined. I saw no need to tell them that GEM allowed none of their personnel to drink alcohol. I spent about thirty minutes butchering the German language in my pathetic attempt to share the Gospel the first time in German, but I left them with my New Testament. They thanked me when I finished my deadly drink. I shook everyone's hand and said goodbye. I had fallen in love with Europe. I stepped out of that bar knowing that I would never finish my PhD in physics.

I returned to Bible college in the fall and met Christine. She avoided me that first year because others had warned her to stay away from The Soldier. I had caused quite a bit of consternation during my freshman year questioning all the legalism, so the administration "requested" that I live with the missions professor in his basement. I should write a book about my second year in college.

Both the professor and I survived that year, and, the following summer, I met two societal outcasts, who talked me into living with them in a rickety old cabin in the woods together. The owner charged no rent because he just wanted it inhabited for the summer. He had put in plumbing and electricity but had kept the outdoor outhouse. He didn't want any vagabonds moving in until he could renovate it as a rental during the ski season. Lots of tourists hit the ski slopes in that area in the winter. I enjoyed that summer of shooting rats out of the walls and driving to the East Coast for a SCUBA trip, but by late August I was ready for the classroom again. The administration moved me back into the dorm. I think that the missions professor had given up trying to reform me.

Then I met a new Vietnam Vet who came as a freshman.

The school had renovated some World War II military barracks into our dorm rooms. Those barracks had been used to imprison Japanese prisoners of war captured in the Pacific. We felt fortunate that all the locks had been removed. My dorm room, at the end of the hall next to an exit door, held a bunk bed, a small desk, a chair, a small dresser and a standing cabinet for some hanging clothes. I bumped into some piece of furniture every time I turned around. I loved it. I didn't have to share a room with anyone. The guys in the other rooms kept asking me to turn down my rock and roll music. They considered me an almost pagan.

The Vet moved in two rooms down the hall. One night, after midnight, I heard some noise outside my room that did not sound like someone was going to the bathroom. Then I heard the exit door close too quietly. I got up, dressed and quietly snuck out to quell my curiosity. The Vet had dressed in full camouflage fatigues and was heading up the ridge behind the barracks. It took just a few seconds to realize that he was reconnoitering the entire area. He did that a couple nights in a row.

I knew that he had to sleep sometime, so I assumed that he slept before and after his recon trips. After his third or fourth night, I jammed some pieces of wood between his room's one window and the outside window sill, so he couldn't open it from the inside. Then I waited until he went to sleep, and I tied a rope to his door knob and anchored the rope to the bathroom door across the hall. He couldn't open his door without making a lot of noise, the major sin of a recon man. Then I quietly took a blanket and pillow and laid down on the hall floor and went to sleep. When he woke up and tried to open his door, I softly called his name and told him that there would be no recon patrol tonight, that he should go back to sleep, and that we would talk at breakfast.

The next morning, I made it to breakfast before he did. He entered the dining hall looking for the enemy. I had shooed other guys away from sitting with me for breakfast, and as he approached my table, I raised my hand to hold him off and said quietly, "I followed you for two nights, and you never knew it. Who's the better man?" He stopped a few feet away from the table. I said, "Go get some food. Let's talk." He had relaxed somewhat when he returned with a tray of food. We talked.

He had been on a Long Range Recon Patrol (LRRP) his entire time in Nam. He claimed that his team had received extremely specific training, much more intensive than the other teams, and that he and his team had been in the field for eighteen months. He was team leader. Their mission was to stay deep in the jungle long enough to be overlooked and to keep sending intel back as long as possible. They were not to engage the enemy unless their lives were in danger, or if they could completely destroy that enemy, so the enemy could not report their existence to their superiors. Gather intel and do not be detected by the Vietcong.

Then, one day, they were spotted by the Vietcong. They only realized it when he saw a Vietcong give a live grenade to a three-year-old Vietnamese girl and motion for her to give that gift to her American friends. She started walking toward his team. If she got too close, the grenade could be dropped and the girl and his men would be wounded or killed. He shot her, and she blew up. They were deep in the jungle and then they ran for their lives. They almost got wasted, but one of our ships off the coast managed to dig some very deep holes with some very large shells that they placed between them and the pursuing Vietcong. That had been less than a year ago.

At school, only one other person knew his story. The Dean of the Faculty. I told the Dean that the Vet had told me what happened. The Dean had three small daughters. He began asking the Vet to babysit evenings while the Dean and his wife went out together. Over the next two years, we continued to reminisce. He healed. He eventually married a beautiful lady, had three daughters of his own and spent a number of years in Venezuela as a missionary. Years later, we connected again, and he informed me that he still loved the jungle. I told him that he needed counseling.

12. The Answer I Found

I've read a number of books by authors who wrote of their experiences in Vietnam—both enlisted men and officers, soldiers who knew nothing more than that they needed to shoot the enemy, and well-informed intelligence officers who were given the bigger picture of at least their part of the war.

Most of them have expressed the terror of the minute-by-minute exposure to death. No one was immune from the constant fear of death, because no one was safe. This war did not kill you "en masse" like the major battles of Verdun in the World War I or D-Day in World War II. In a jungle war, the enemy is everywhere all the time, and soldiers died one at a time. We knew that we could be killed in any given second and in a variety of ways. There was no visible coherent system of existence that regulated each person's death, and that made every death appear to be senselessly random. Reason didn't help because there were no human rules to be evaluated. It was mind-numbing to even think about it.

The human brain needs order. In combat, everyone builds their own fantasy world. They fight to build a coherent system of do's and don'ts. Keep your weapon clean, stay alert (even when you were sleeping), never take a risk that isn't attached to an order from a superior. If you do everything right (what the hell did that mean?), you'll get out alive.

Then why did that soldier get killed who followed all those rules? The good guy and the scumbag died right next to each other. Both dead. Living a perfect life and killing the enemy guaranteed nothing.

Some soldier-philosophers began to wonder if the dead were dying as some kind of exchange sacrifice, that the other person died in your place. Some speculated that maybe a person doesn't have a right to live out a full life. Everybody dies someday, so why should a person get to choose his own death day?

We coped by keeping our minds off those questions. Just do your job and keep waking up the next morning. But a person can't stop thinking about the most important thing in his life: his life. Most everyone resorted to some form of superstition and carried a corresponding physical artifact on their person.

"If I have a fiancé at home, that gives me the right to stay alive."

Some guys were devastated to receive "Dear John" letters from their fiancés after just a few months in Nam. It was a horrible feeling to realize that your reason for staying alive depended on someone who broke her promise to stay faithful to you until you returned home, alive or in a body-bag.

"My grandmother gave me a silver ring engraved with the words, 'live well' on it. That will protect me." The engraving probably should have read, "Count your days."

"A cross is the most religious sign in the Western world. I wear one around my next for security." But Vietnam lies in the Eastern world, and you needed to keep the cross under your shirt, so that the light bouncing off it wouldn't make you the perfect target for a sniper's bullet.

No one could rationally explain how their treasured piece of superstition would protect them. You just had to believe, man! I found it almost hilarious, but sad, that humans need something to believe in, but they usually gravitate to something below themselves, like a piece of inanimate dead metal.

On one mission, a GI got shot in the chest. When the firefight was over, and we reached his position, he had taken off his gear and was rummaging through his vest pocket. He pulled out a Gideon New Testament. The bullet was lodged in that New Testament. I have no idea why it did not penetrate that small book. After that the soldier begged or borrowed any and all Gideon New Testaments he could get, and he put them in every pocket all over his body. A good luck charm. I doubt he ever read one, but that's my pessimism surfacing.

Eventually, I found the answer. It turned out to be quite simple, but a person has to be desperate enough to look at the two options: we don't know or the one I'm giving you now.

Our minds can never arrive at a logical answer because we don't have all the information. God created reason and placed reason in the mind of human beings, but God didn't create beings equal to Himself, i.e., giving us His omniscience (knowing everything). God knows why He chose to create a person and then take that person's life back, but since God is not under our authority, He has chosen to not answer our question of why did I not die and the other person did.

If there is no all-knowing God, there is no answer to that question. Period. I spoke about the resurrection of Jesus with a soldier once. He said he couldn't understand how God could put all those body parts back together ten thousand years later. He wanted to know how God could keep track of everything.

"That's extremely simply," I replied. "God knows everything. Even at the human level, we realize that the person who has all the facts is in the best position to know how to get things done. The more information I have, the better I can keep track of everything. And only a supernatural Being knows everything."

He just shook his head and turned away. He chose to hang onto his good luck charm and hope that it would save his life.

God wanted me to live for some purpose in the future, and God took the other guy, and God has never chosen to tell me why. Since I can't see the whole picture about my own life, I've never been burdened to figure out another person's journey on this earth or that person's eternity.

Many soldiers have written that they went to Vietnam with no purpose in life to begin with. And when they came home, they came back with the additional baggage of that nagging question—"Why did I live?"—but they returned to resume their same purposeless lives as before.

Because many people have no purpose in this life, they are asking the wrong question. They should ask: If I have no purpose in life, why shouldn't I die? Not, why did I live, but, why didn't I die? But shouldn't I stay alive to keep my loved ones, as few as they may be, from experiencing the sadness of my death? Why? Why should our loved ones be allowed to keep on living? Does the length of our lives really matter? A shorter life with purpose can impact others far more than a longer life can without purpose. A life without purpose rarely impacts anyone. So the length of our life is irrelevant. It's what we do with the time we've been given. The purpose of our life outshines the length of our lives.

We may even proclaim that we have purpose in our lives, but without being connected to our Creator, why is He obligated to allow us to live a long life, regardless of the purpose we have chosen for ourselves? If we are connected to our Creator, then staying alive longer serves to carry out His purpose in our lives. When that purpose is over, it's time to go home.

If there is a Creator, then we might want to consult Him about what He wants from us in this life, since He determines how long or short our life will be.

If there is no Creator, then the entire discussion becomes a waste of time, since there is no "logical" answer to the question. If there is no life after death with the Creator, then our purposeless lives are erased from our memories when we die. And there is no one to consult.

I get very emotional when I see the suffering that goes on in the world, but I don't regret nor feel guilty when I don't suffer or die like others. I'm not insensitive, cold-hearted, or mindless. Since I lay no claim to omniscience, I will let God answer that question, which He won't do, because He is not obligated to do so to any of His created beings. Since humans, in comparison with God, are extremely limited in their overall knowledge of everything, it is highly unlikely that they would even be able to understand God's answer anyway. I choose to not feel guilty about something I can't understand nor do anything about. God has His own reasons for what He does.

Jesus has used my Vietnam experiences a number of times since 1969, but I will close this book with one last story.

Christine was born in Upstate New York. She claims to have been quite precocious as a child. When she was six years old, she would come home from church, set up her dolls all in a row and would play church by singing and preaching to them. She attended a summer camp when she was ten, became a follower of Jesus and felt that Jesus wanted her to become a missionary when she grew up. That same year her dad left, and she didn't see him again for nineteen years.

Partially due to her family's poverty, she found herself at the bottom of the social ladder in high school. Her grades suffered because she had to help her mother to raise her two younger sisters until she left for college. Those years challenged her faith in Jesus, but instead of giving up, those trials strengthened her desire to serve Him fully.

One day in June, 1967, when she was days away from turning sixteen, she turned on the evening news. The newsman announced that war was imminent in the Middle East, and that American paratroopers had just loaded onto transport planes and were waiting for orders to fly to the Middle East to parachute into combat in order to defend Israel. That newscast impelled her to think about her own future. She began praying for her future husband—whomever he might be. Her future husband might be sitting in one of those planes, waiting for those orders.

The next year, in 1968, a young man from Woodland Park, Colorado, went to Vietnam as a soldier. He came back in a casket. His death devastated the entire community. The impact of his death made Christine wonder if her future husband might not be in Vietnam right at that time. She continued to pray for her future husband. She prayed for him in Vietnam sometime between February and May of that year, 1968.

During her senior year, she visited Rockmont College in Denver seeking a good fit for her goals. She was looking for Bible and missions, but she was disappointed when the faculty only emphasized their upcoming accreditation, which she didn't understand. She then attended "College Daze" at Western Bible Institute (WBI) in Denver, and the word accreditation never came up. They talked about the fundamental importance of the Bible for any profession, and especially for missions. She enrolled immediately.

She arrived at WBI in the fall of 1970. She met her future husband at WBI. He had gotten wounded the first time in February and three times on the same day in May, 1968. She married him on May 19, 1973. I am eternally grateful for her prayers.

More Books by Floyd

Evangelism for the Fainthearted
Paperback, Kindle, Audible.com

Mark Challenges the Aeneid
Wipf & Stock Publishers
Paperback

Historical Books by Christine

In the Shadow of the Cathedral
Paperback and Kindle

Hammering at the Doors of Heaven
Paperback and Kindle

Malachi Commentary by Christine

What Price Sacrifice
Paperback and Kindle

As of 2020, connect with Floyd and Christine:

<u>Website</u>: www.floydschneider.com
Online Courses:
    www.tradewindswest.teachable.com
<u>Youtube channel</u>: Youtube.com, then
    floydschneider.com
<u>Great Northern University</u> (GNU),
    https://greatnorthernu.org